TEA PARTY TIME

Romantic Quilts & Tasty Tidbits

That Patchwork Place ®

Nancy J. Martin

CREDITS

Photography . . . . .Doug Plager
Illustration and Graphics . . . . .Sandra Dean
Joanne Lauterjung
Text and Cover Design . . . . .Joanne Lauterjung
Editor . . . . .Barbara Weiland
Copy Editor . . . . .Liz McGehee

Tea Party Time: Romantic Quilts and Tasty Tidbits©
©1992 by Nancy J. Martin

That Patchwork Place, Inc., PO Box 118, Bothell, WA 98041-0118

Printed in the British Crown Colony of Hong Kong
97 96 95 94 93   6 5 4 3

The information in this book is presented in good faith, but no warranty is given nor results guaranteed. Since That Patchwork Place, Inc., has no control over choice of materials or procedures, the company assumes no responsibility for the use of this data.

Library of Congress Cataloging-in-Publication Data

Martin, Nancy J.
    Tea part time : romantic quilts and tasty tidbits / Nancy J. Martin ; [editor, Barbara Weiland].
       p. cm.
    ISBN 1-56477-008-7:
    1. Patchwork—Patterns. 2. Appliqué. I. Weiland, Barbara.
    II. Title.
TT835.M3833 1992   92-44945
746.46—dc20   CIP

Published in the United States of America

Contents

Introduction 5
General Directions 6
Supplies 6
Stain Removal 8
Fabric Overdyeing 8
Embroidery Stitches 9
Ribbon Couching 9
Lace Collage 10
Quilts and Wall Hangings 11
    Tea Party© 13
    Tea Baskets 17
    Doily Basket 21
    Handkerchief Basket 25
    Dresden Plate 28
    Fantastic Fans 30
    A Doll's Tea Party 34
    Catnip Tea 37
    Japanese Tea Ceremony 41
    Plaid Pines 43
Special Projects 47
    Kitchen Cats 47
    Bridal Pillow 50
    Tea Cozy 51
Glossary of Techniques 54
Recipes 59

Photo courtesy of Jeannie Van Hoff, Richland, Wash.

Young ladies were taught to "hem their day with prayer,
so that it would be less likely to unravel before nightfall."

DEDICATION

To my grandmothers, Margaret Butler Parry, who taught me the many joys of embroidery and stitching when I was just a little girl; and Marcella Reinhardt Ruffing, who made the only quilt that survived from my ancestors.

ACKNOWLEDGMENTS

My deep appreciation goes to:

Mimi Dietrich, Catonsville, Maryland, for use of her Tea Party quilt.

Judy Pollard, Seattle, Washington, for use of her Fan Tan Fantasy and Fantastic Fans quilts.

Mary Ann Farmer, Deephaven, Minnesota, for use of her cat pattern in Kitchen Cats and Catnip Tea.

Merlin Sampson, Palmerston North, New Zealand, for use of her Kimono pattern in Japanese Tea Ceremony.

Marsha McCloskey, Seattle, Washington, for use of her Tea Cozy design.

Marta Estes, Beverly Payne, and Freda Smith, for their fine hand quilting.

Joan Hanson, who lent me her lovely yellow Fiesta Ware.

Bev Murrish, for making a delicious Buche de Noel and Teacup Petits Fours to be photographed and consumed.

The Pleasant Company, P.O. Box 497, Middleton, WI 53562-9440, who provided new outfits for Kirsten, Samantha, and Molly for the doll's tea party.

Gladys Shipek, for finding so many wonderful pieces of lace at bargain prices.

My parents, William and Ida J. Ruffing, who entrusted me with my grandmother's Dresden Plate quilt.

Introduction

The tea party is a lovely ritual that is again gaining favor as an entertaining way to spend time with one's special friends and acquaintances. Its popularity was at a peak during Victorian times, when young ladies enjoyed the gentle pleasures of taking afternoon tea with friends, often bringing along handwork and stitching, while exchanging patterns, recipes, and gossip. It has been said that the ladies' tongues were as sharp as their needles on those afternoons. In defense of the gossip, it served a useful purpose, for it helped define the limits of acceptable behavior for a lady.

Nonetheless, ladies enjoyed this afternoon entertainment and all of its trappings. There were tea cloths and napkins, embellished with delicate embroidery and lace, on a small tea table. Since tea was a special occasion, it was usually served in the front parlor, where fine needlework pillows, samplers, and piano cloths were on display for guests to admire.

As customs and decorating styles changed, many of the linens that were once used abundantly in the home fell out of favor. Thus, lovely embroidered pillowcases, dresser scarves, tea cloths, napkins, and card-table covers, made by grandmothers and aunts, remain in drawers or trunks. Others, stained by age and use, meet an inglorious end at flea markets or garage sales, where they are sold from crumpled cardboard boxes for ridiculously low prices. I always consider it my personal mission to rescue these items and recycle them into projects that are worthy of the original needlewoman's stitches. This was my inspiration for *Tea Party Time*.

As this theme began to form, I wanted to incorporate even more aspects of the tea party into this book. For this reason, all of the quilts and projects have been photographed in a special setting in my "front parlor." This allows me to share my collection of teapots, which I have been acquiring over the last four years. The teapots include antique porcelain, current collectible china, special mementos purchased while visiting other countries, and even one shaped like a sewing machine.

I've included menu ideas for each tea party and three pages of pullout recipes, beginning on page 59, a throwback to the recipes exchanged at those Victorian tea parties. As for the gossip, I'll leave that to your quilt group or sewing circle, when you share your own hand-stitched creations from *Tea Party Time*.

Nancy

General Directions

For every quilt or craft project, read through the list of materials needed before you begin. Gather the necessary materials and become familiar with all the directions before you proceed. Examine photographs and illustrations to see what an item looks like when completed.

Templates and pattern pieces are full size, so it won't be necessary to graph or enlarge patterns. Dimensions, rather than pattern pieces, are given for patterns that are a simple square, rectangle, triangle, or circle. *Do not add seam allowances to these measurements; they are already included.* Cut pieces the exact size given.

Do not cut templates or pattern pieces from the book or you will destroy text and patterns on the reverse side. Instead, make templates or trace patterns onto tissue paper, making sure to include all lines and markings.

All seams are ¼" wide, and all fabrics are sewn together with right sides of fabric facing, unless otherwise indicated.

All fabric requirements are based on 42 usable inches across the width of the fabric after 44"/45"-wide yardage is washed and pressed. If you do not have 42 usable inches after washing, you may need to purchase additional fabrics.

Several quilts have a materials specification, which lists 1½ yards of assorted yellow prints or 1 yard assorted red and green prints. This means you need to purchase yellow prints in varying amounts to equal 1½ yards. If you use six yellow prints, purchase ¼ yard of each; or purchase ⅜ yard of 4 fabrics; or ½ yard of 3 fabrics. For the second example, fabric purchases should add up to a total of 1 yard of assorted red and green prints; do not purchase one yard of red prints and one yard of green prints. Remember to purchase less yardage if you are also utilizing scraps.

In many cases, you will need only a scrap of fabric for your project. You may use any suitable fabric scrap on hand. The materials lists for these projects indicate that ⅛ yard of fabric is necessary because that is the least amount of fabric you can buy. You can expect to have fabric left over.

Specific directions for using the quilt patterns are on page 11. There is also a Glossary of Techniques on pages 54–58 with machine-piecing tips and complete directions for quilt finishing.

Supplies

BACKGROUND FABRICS

For the background fabric, select a firmly woven fabric that is compatible with the embellished items in color, texture, and weave. A fine, white Pima cotton works well with delicate, finely woven lace tablecloths and linens. Linen fabric would be an appropriate choice for heavier-weight, embroidered dresser scarves or napkins. A muslin background fabric coordinates with coarser embroidered items. Use 100 percent cotton prints as the background for quilt blocks.

Preshrink all fabrics. Test for colorfastness. Do not use any fabric you think might run. Don't avoid prewashing because you prefer to work on "fresh fabric" or because you plan to have the item dry-cleaned. Remember, colors in fabric may run if they get wet accidentally.

EMBELLISHED ITEMS

New Linens, Tablecloths, Doilies, Place Mats, and Napkins. A wide variety of imported linens are available in cutwork lace and Battenberg lace styles. These linens can often be found in fabric and craft stores at a reasonable price, making their inclusion in quilting and craft projects feasible.

Used Linens, Tablecloths, Dresser Scarves, Napkins, and Patchwork Blocks. Incorporate used linens in your project only if (1) the fabric is firmly woven and shows no weak or worn areas from use; (2) embroidery stitches are secure and all knots are firmly in place; (3) lace trims and edgings are intact.

Coordinating sets of dresser scarves or tablecloths and napkins are good purchases, since you will often find the fabrics, edges, trims, and motifs in varying sizes. Don't hesitate to purchase stained or torn linens for your projects. (You can recycle them into your projects by using the stain-removal tips on page 8.) If stains cannot be removed, cover them with button clusters, embroidery stitches, or ribbon couching. (See pages 8–10.)

RIBBONS AND TRIMS

Both old and new ribbons and trims may be incorporated into your designs. Laces or crocheted edgings, such as those made for pillowcases, work especially well. Save edgings from damaged or used linens; they may be sewn into the seam like piping or used to border another linen.

BUTTONS

Special decorative buttons add interest to your designs. Button clusters (page 8) can be used to hide stains or add sparkle to an unembellished area. Antique or used buttons that are finely detailed and highly decorative are good choices.

Button Clusters. Add dimension and interest to a project with "button clusters." Gather an assortment of buttons in various sizes, shapes, and color shadings. White, ivory, and off-white buttons work well together. Include shank, two-hole, and four-hole styles.

Begin by stitching the largest button for the center of the button cluster. Working from the center toward outer edges, hand stitch buttons in place, gradually decreasing button size.

SORTING AND STORING SUPPLIES

Launder and treat all used linens for stains before using. (See Stain Removal tips below.) Many old linens have a musty smell, which will be objectionable while you work on the item or when the item is used. Press linens while slightly damp and fold loosely. Try not to fold along original fold lines, or more stress and soil will be added to these areas.

Sort used linens by the color of the embellishment, not by the type of item or base fabric. Store in containers with other items featuring embroidery or crocheted edging in that color. Use one container for pink, another container for blue, another for lavender, for example. I also have a container for all-white embellished items. Plastic see-through storage boxes, plastic dishpans, wicker baskets, or wire mesh baskets all make suitable containers for storage.

In an open closet or cupboard, wicker baskets or hampers may also be used to store linens. These baskets are both decorative and add needed storage space.

Stain Removal

Small lace items can be laundered in a jar. Baste lace to a piece of clean cloth and place in a large screw-top jar containing soap flakes dissolved in hot water. Screw on cap and shake jar vigorously. Let stand and then repeat several times, if necessary. Finally, rinse thoroughly in several changes of clear, warm water, still using the jar. Remove lace from mounting cloth and pin out to shape on a flat cotton pad, using rustproof pins. When lace is completely dry, press with a warm iron through several layers of muslin.[1]

Stains on linens and lace are best treated individually. Never use chlorine bleach or oxalic acid. Sodium perborate, available at drugstores, will remove some stains. Hydrogen peroxide is useful for removing stains from silk lace. Treat rust stains with a paste made from baking soda, or cream of tartar, and water. To remove mildew, try sodium perborate or baking soda.

Fabric Overdyeing

If stains are not removable, you may want to achieve an "antique" look by overdyeing or staining the fabric. Or you may want to use staining to tone down

1. "Looking After Beautiful Things," *Golden Hands Magazine* (London: Marshall Cavendish, Ltd., 1972).

the whiteness or brightness of fabric, lace, or crochet work. The best method I've found for staining fabric is to use a coffee solution.

1. Put 2 tablespoons instant coffee in a medium-sized bowl. Add enough boiling water in bowl to submerge fabric and stir. Let cool.
2. Soak fabric 1–2 hours. Wring excess coffee water from fabric. For delicate items, gently blot out excess moisture in terrycloth towels.
3. Put fabric into dryer and dry. The heat from the dryer will set the stains.
4. Iron the fabric to prepare for use.

Embroidery Stitches

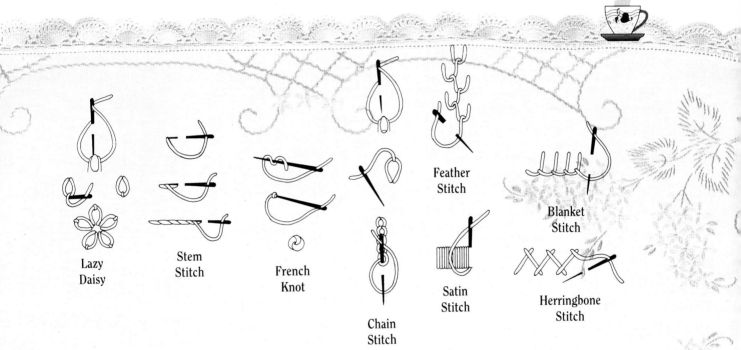

Lazy Daisy

Stem Stitch

French Knot

Chain Stitch

Feather Stitch

Satin Stitch

Blanket Stitch

Herringbone Stitch

Use a sharp needle and two strands of embroidery floss for each stitch.

Ribbon Couching

Determine position of ribbon. Mark at equal intervals (½"–¾" apart). Layer ⅛"-wide ribbon over ¼"-wide ribbon. Lay ribbons over marking, leaving a 2" length at the beginning.

With needle and thread, make several tiny straight stitches at each marking, pinching ribbons tightly together. Knot thread after stitching at each mark, but do not cut. Stitch at next mark, leaving a little slack in the ribbon so it will puff.

Leave another short length at end of ribbon. Add a bow at both ends to hide ribbon raw edges.

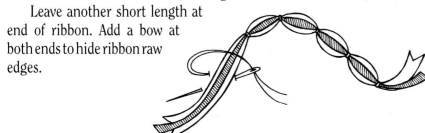

Lace Collage

Laces and trims selected for a lace collage should blend well in both color and texture. A perfect match is neither necessary nor desirable. Include a variety of laces and trims to add interest. Look for interesting shapes and effects. If you cannot find enough old trims, intermix some new trims and bridal appliqués. Give new pieces a vintage look by soaking them in a coffee solution. (See steps 1–4 on page 9.)

Doilies in a variety of sizes and shapes work well in lace collage. Doilies should be sewn in place by hand with tiny stitches. All points and corners of the design should be tacked down securely to preserve the lace and allow it to be removed at a later time, if desired.

It may be necessary to cut a damaged doily or piece of lace to utilize it in a design. Machine stitch around the area to be cut, being careful not to pull or distort design. Make a second row of stitching close to the first and cut carefully between the lines of stitching. This keeps doilies, laces, and crocheted pieces from disintegrating once they are cut.

Decorative corners from handkerchiefs, napkins, and dresser scarves are good choices for lace collage. Trim away the excess handkerchief, dresser scarf, or napkin fabric to minimize bulkiness.

For the background, select a solid-colored fabric or very muted print to show off the lace to its best advantage. Moiré taffeta is a nice choice since it also adds apparent textural as well as visual interest. You can make attractive lace collages using a damaged quilt (especially a crazy quilt) as the background fabric. Use doilies, ribbons, fabric yo-yos, laces, and button clusters to hide damaged areas.

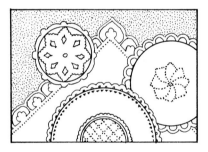

Begin by positioning the largest design pieces or those with a more solid background first. Overlap with doilies and smaller, more delicate pieces. Blend open areas together with ribbons and laces.

Take your time and experiment with the trims. Move them around until you find an arrangement that pleases you. Don't fight the design elements, but utilize their lines to best advantage. Some doily shapes may suggest baskets or fans to be incorporated into a design.

When you are pleased with a design, pin design elements in place, then tack down by hand. Take tiny stitches, making sure no raw edges are exposed and all design elements are secured.

Embellish lace collage with ribbon couching (page 9) or button clusters (page 8). These embellishments can tie the design together and add textural interest while disguising flaws or damaged areas.

Quilts and Wall Hangings

This section of the book contains directions and templates for ten different wall hangings and quilts. The patterns are graded as to difficulty:

Beginner

Intermediate

Advanced

Use this information to select a project in keeping with your skills.

All templates for pieced blocks are labeled with the template number, block name, and number of pieces to cut for one block, except for the overall patterns. Templates for borders and set pieces indicate the number of pieces to cut for the entire quilt. "Cut 1 + 1R" will sometimes appear on a template, indicating that the template should be reversed so that a mirror-image shape is cut. Cut the first piece with the template face up and then flip it over to cut the reversed piece.

On each template, reference is also made to the fabric to be used. This is meant to help you identify template pieces and relate them to the finished quilts. Do not let this labeling restrict your design; feel free to substitute your own colorations to achieve more individual results.

Where necessary, shapes are marked with a grain line. All templates, except those needed for appliqué, include ¼"-wide seam allowances. Appliqué templates are numbered in their order of application.

Several of the quilts are Template-Free™ and incorporate the timesaving technique of cutting bias squares. Consult the Glossary of Techniques on pages 54–58 to familiarize yourself with this method.

Border strips should always be cut from yardage before the templates are cut, ensuring that continuous yardage is available for the border strips. If border strips must be pieced, seams should be pressed open and placed in the center of each side of the quilt for minimum visibility.

Consult the Glossary of Techniques for machine-piecing tips and complete directions for quilt finishing.

This Tea Party Friendship quilt, made by Mimi Dietrich of Catonsville, Maryland, evokes memories as warm as a cup of hot tea and a lovely letter from a dear friend. Friendship signatures are hidden in the steam above the teacups. Teacup Petits Fours (recipe on page 63) make a welcome snack while catching up on correspondence.

Fabric Selection: This friendship quilt features a chintz teapot surrounded by eight teacups, which have signatures hidden in the swirls of steam. Select a large-scale chintz for the teapot and wide border, a coordinating small print for the teacups, and a solid color accent for the saucers, narrow border, and binding. Muslin or a soft-print background will allow the signatures to be easily read.

Materials: 44"-wide fabric
   ¾ yd. solid or soft-print fabric for background
   ⅝ yd. large floral print for teapot and wide border
   ¼ yd. small print for teacups
   ⅝ yd. solid accent fabric for saucers, narrow border, and binding
   1 yd. fabric for backing
   Pilot SC-UF ultra-fine point, permanent marking pen
   Silver fabric marking pencil
   Batting and thread to finish

Cutting

1. From solid background fabric, cut 9 squares, each 8½" x 8½". (An optional method can be used to avoid seams between blocks: Cut a 24½" square of background fabric. Mark the 8" squares on the fabric, leaving ¼"-wide seam allowances around the outside edges.)
2. From accent fabric, cut 4 strips, each 1¼" x 45", for the narrow borders.
3. From large floral print, cut 4 strips, each 3½" x 45", for the wide borders.
4. Save the remaining fabric for the appliqués.

DIRECTIONS

1. Using the teacup and teapot patterns on pages 15 and 16, center the squares of background fabric on the patterns. Using a silver marking pencil, trace the appliqué placement lines onto the fabric squares for 8 Teacup blocks and 1 Teapot block.
2. Following the paper-patch appliqué directions on page 56, cut teacups and teapot from fabric, prepare, and position on background squares.
3. For the teacup handles:
   Cut 8 bias strips, each ¾" x 5", from accent fabric, using a rotary cutter and a clear plastic ruler. Fold the strips in half lengthwise, wrong sides together, and press with a steam iron. Position the raw edges of the strip on the outer marked teacup handle line with the folded edge covering the inside line. Using small running stitches, stitch the strip to the background through the center of the strip. Roll the folded edge over the seam allowance. Appliqué the fold to the background fabric to create a smooth, even handle.
4. Appliqué the teacups and teapot to the background squares, following the numbered sequence noted on the pattern.

Dimensions: 32" x 32"

Teacup block, 8"

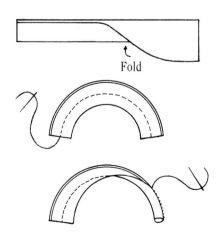

Teapot block, 8"

Fold

5. For the signatures on the Teacup blocks:
   Place the appliquéd Teacup block on top of the pattern. Using the Pilot SC-UF ultra-fine point permanent pen, trace the "steam" curls. Using the straight lines for a guide, sign your name in the center of the cup, adding a small curl to the end. You may want to practice on a sheet of paper before writing on fabric. A small piece of freezer paper ironed to the back of your fabric will keep it from slipping as you write.

6. Stitch the 9 blocks together as shown in the piecing diagram, using ¼"-wide seam allowances. Press the seams open.

7. To add the narrow borders, first stitch a 1¼"-wide accent strip to each side of the quilt top. Press the seams toward the accent strips and trim the ends even with the blocks. Then, stitch the other 2 strips to the top and bottom of the quilt top, pressing and trimming as before.

8. To add the wide borders, first stitch a 3½"-wide floral strip to each side of the quilt top. Press the seams toward the accent strips and trim the ends even with the quilt top. Then, stitch the other 2 strips to the top and bottom of the quilt top, pressing and trimming as before.

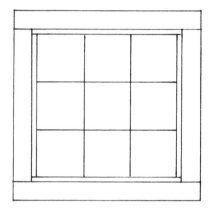

9. Layer with batting and backing, then quilt or tie.

10. Bind with bias strips of fabric.

Quilting Suggestion: Outline quilt around the edges of the teacups and teapot. Quilt a diagonal grid through the background fabric, but not through the teacups and teapot.

#2

#3

#4

#1

#5

Teapot Appliqué Placement

Teacup Appliqué Placement

Dimensions: 44" x 55¼"

Fabric Selection: Tea napkins with cutwork, crocheted detail, and edging or embroidered corners are the basis of this Basket block. Strips for the handle and triangles for the basket base can be cut from the remainder of the napkin. Select a pastel background fabric that will not overpower the delicate stitches of the handwork. Corners of tatted handkerchiefs may be substituted for the tea napkins.

Materials: 44"-wide fabric
    2½ yds. blue print for background, borders, and binding
    ½ yd. white or ecru fabric for basket handles and basket bases
    1¾ yds. fabric for backing
    12 tea napkins or handkerchiefs with fancy edges
    Batting and thread to finish

Basket block, 8"

DIRECTIONS

1. From the lengthwise grain of fabric, cut and set aside:
   2 strips, each 5¼" x 45¾", for side borders;
   2 strips, each 5¼" x 44", for top and bottom borders.
2. Cut 12 Basket blocks from fabrics specified on the template found on page 20. Cut 12 napkin or handkerchief corners so short sides measure 7".
3. Piece 12 Basket blocks:
a. Piece lower portion of Basket block.

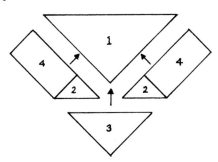

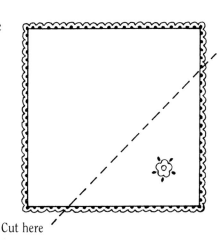

Cut here

b. Position handkerchief or napkin corner on top of Template #1. Pin or baste, then stitch in place by machine. Trim upper edges even with the top of Template #1.

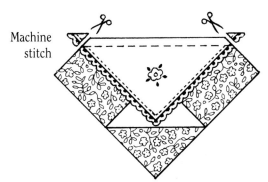

Machine
stitch

A lovely blue Tea Basket quilt, featuring corners from old tea napkins, decorates the wall behind the wicker sofa. A Royal Copenhagen tea service makes an elegant presentation for the Peach Clafouti (recipe on page 59). Quilted by Freda Smith.

c. Cut a 2" x 11" bias strip from matching white or ecru fabric for basket handle. Fold with wrong sides together and stitch ¼" from raw edges. Press bias strip so that seam allowance is centered on the back side of completed handle.

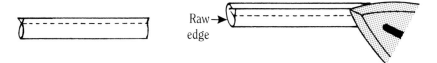

d. Position bias strip for handle on Template #1 and appliqué in place.

e. Join upper and lower portions of Basket block.

4. Cut the following setting triangles from background fabric:
   a. For side setting triangles, cut 3 squares, each 12⅝" x 12⅝". Cut squares twice diagonally to yield 12 triangles. Only 10 are needed.
   b. For corner setting triangles, cut 2 squares, each 6½" x 6½". Cut squares once diagonally to yield 4 triangles.
   c. For alternate blocks, cut 6 squares, each 8½" x 8½".

5. Using the piecing diagram as a guide, stitch Basket blocks, alternate blocks, and setting triangles into diagonal rows. Stitch rows together to form quilt top.

6. Stitch borders to sides, then to top and bottom of quilt top.

7. Layer with batting and backing, then quilt or tie.

8. Bind with bias strips of fabric.

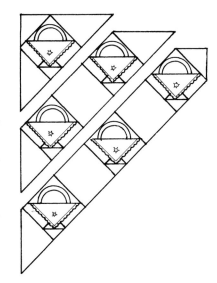

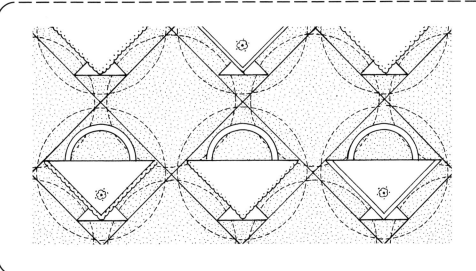

Quilting Suggestion: Quilt large circles approximately 10" in diameter around each basket, positioning circles so that an interlocking design is formed.

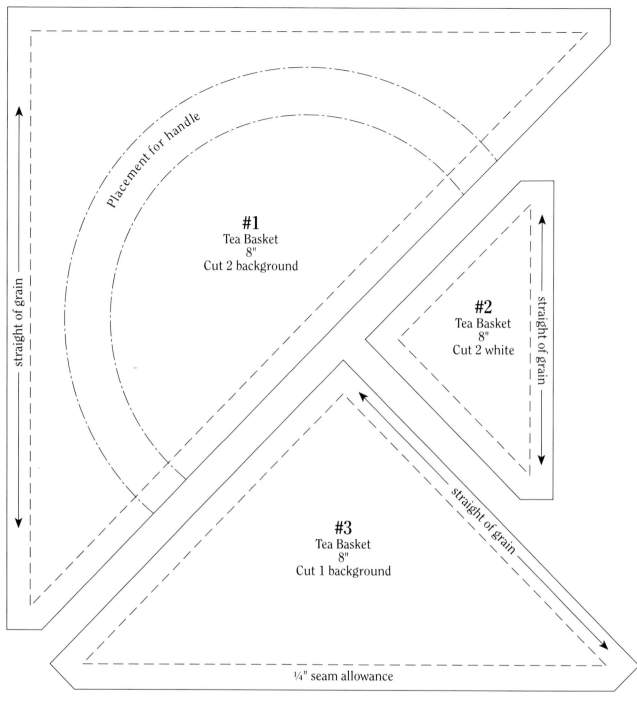

Placement for handle

straight of grain

#1
Tea Basket
8"
Cut 2 background

#2
Tea Basket
8"
Cut 2 white

straight of grain

straight of grain

#3
Tea Basket
8"
Cut 1 background

¼" seam allowance

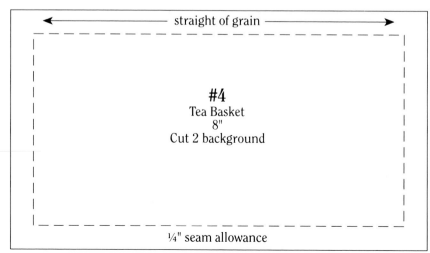

straight of grain

#4
Tea Basket
8"
Cut 2 background

¼" seam allowance

Fabric Selection: Old and new doilies are combined on a pastel background to form flower basket shapes. Don't hesitate to include both white and ecru doilies in the same quilt. A hand-crocheted edging made for pillowcases was used to border the quilt; substitute newly purchased lace trim, if desired. To tone down any of the doilies or trims, soak them in a coffee solution. (See page 9.)

Materials: 44"-wide fabric
    2½ yds. pink print for background, borders, and binding
    ⅜ yd. white or ecru fabric for basket handles
    1⅝ yds. fabric for backing
    6 doilies, 6"–7" in diameter
    5 yds. 2"-wide lace for border trim
    Batting and thread to finish

Dimensions: 41½" x 52¾"

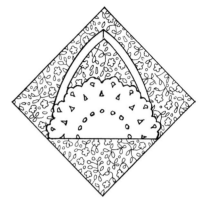

Basket block, 8"

DIRECTIONS

1. From the lengthwise grain of the background fabric, cut and set aside:
    2 strips, each 4" x 45¾", for side borders;
    2 strips, each 4" x 41½", for top and bottom borders.
2. Cut 18 squares, each 8½" x 8½", from background fabric.
3. Carefully cut doilies in half and position on background squares, following the placement diagram on page 24. Baste cut edge of doily in place.
4. Cut 12 bias strips, each 2" x 11", from the white or ecru fabric for basket handles.
5. Fold each strip with wrong sides together and stitch ¼" from raw edges.

6. Press bias strip so that seam allowance is centered on the back side of completed handle.

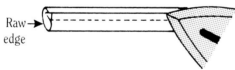
Raw→ edge

7. Position bias strip for handle on background square, trimming to correct length and placing raw edges under doily. Fold upper corner of basket handle as shown.
8. Tack doily to background fabric and appliqué handle in place. Make 12 Doily Basket blocks.
9. Trim away excess fabric so that the cut edge is even with the doily. From the pink print, cut 6 squares, each 5⅞" x 5⅞". Cut squares once diagonally to make 12 triangles. Stitch a triangle to the lower corner of each Basket block.
10. Cut the following setting triangles from background fabric:
    a. For side setting triangles, cut 3 squares, each 12⅝" x 12⅝". Cut squares twice diagonally to yield 12 triangles. Only 10 are needed.

22

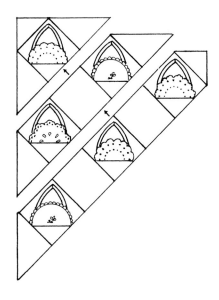

b. For corner setting triangles, cut 2 squares, each 6½" x 6½". Cut squares once diagonally to yield 4 triangles.

11. Using the piecing diagram at left as a guide, stitch Basket blocks, the remaining 6 blocks cut from background fabric, and setting triangles into diagonal rows. Stitch rows together to form quilt top.

12. Baste lace trim to side edges, having raw edges even and finished edge toward quilt top. Add side borders and stitch. Press borders and lace toward outside edge of quilt.

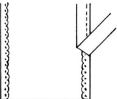

13. Baste lace trim to top and bottom of quilt as above, beginning and ending lace even with the lace edge at each side and folding under raw edges. Add top and bottom borders. Press borders and lace toward outside edge of quilt top.

14. Tack outside edges of lace to border fabric and carefully secure folded raw edges at corners.

15. Layer with batting and backing, then quilt or tie.

16. Bind with bias strips of fabric.

Quilting Suggestion: Outline quilt around each basket shape. Quilt a Baptist fan pattern across quilt top inside of lace, but not through basket. Echo quilt 2 lines of quilting ½" apart along lace edge.

Baptist fan

Echo quilting along lace edge

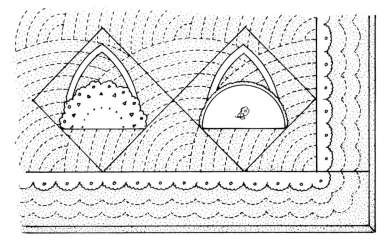

Delicate doilies are fashioned into flower-basket shapes in this softly feminine quilt. Quilted by Beverly Payne. While stitching, guests are served Sour Cream Coffee Cake (recipe on page 59) from the Blue Indies coffee service.

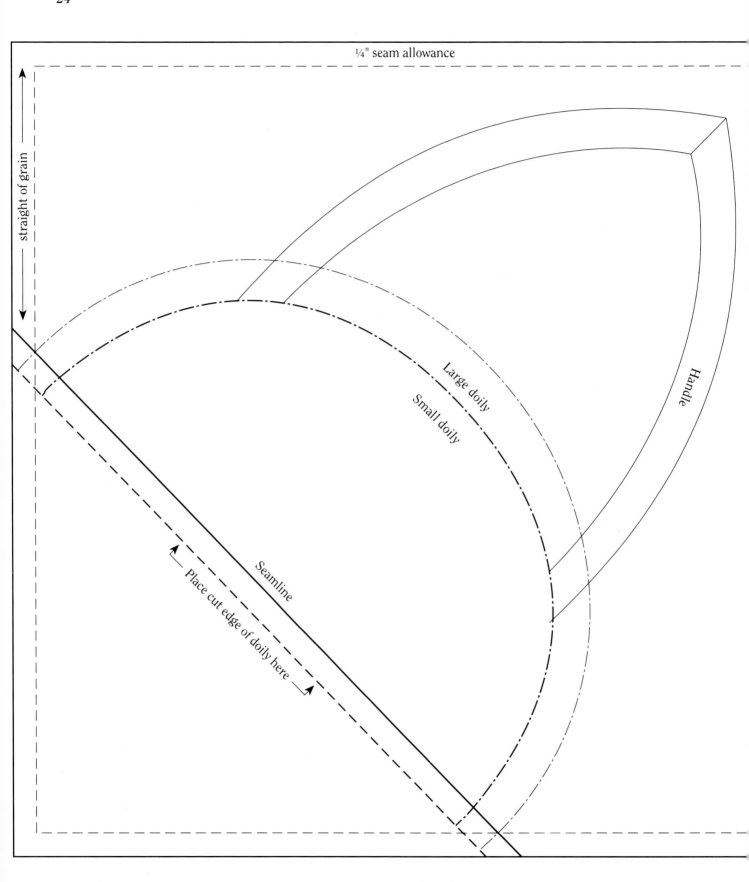

Placement Diagram for Doily Basket

Fabric Selection: Six different yellow prints were selected for the Basket blocks, inspired by Joan Hanson's May Basket design. The center of each basket is filled with flowers from floral handkerchiefs. A large-scale floral print is used for the setting triangles. The two center blocks are done in a white-on-white fabric, which highlights an intricate quilting design.

Materials: 44"-wide fabric

    1½ yds. assorted yellow prints for baskets
    1 yd. white-on-white print for background and alternate blocks
    ⅞ yd. yellow floral print for setting triangles
    ½ yd. yellow print for border (cut crosswise) and binding
    1½ yds. fabric for backing
    6 floral-print handkerchiefs
    Batting and thread to finish

Dimensions: 33" x 47"

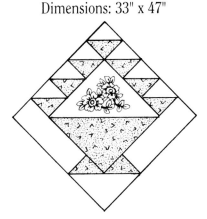

Basket block, 10"

TEMPLATE-FREE™ CUTTING:

From the assorted yellow prints, make bias squares to be used in the piecing of Basket blocks, following directions on pages 55–56. You will need 7 bias squares for each block.

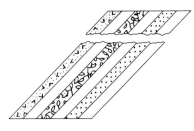

1. Cut a 2½"-wide bias strip from each yellow print. Cut a ½-yard long piece from the white-on-white background fabric, then cut six 2½"-wide bias strips from this. With the yellow print and background strips alternating, stitch them together, using ¼"-wide seams. Press seams toward yellow fabric. Make 2 sets of these strips.
2. Beginning at the lower end of strips, cut the first 2 sides of the bias squares, aligning the 45° marking on the seam line.

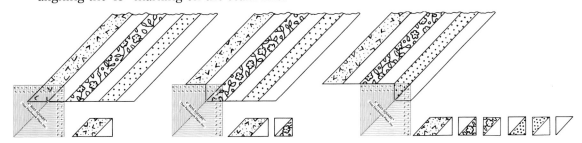

3. Turn cut segments and place Bias Square® on the opposite 2 sides, accurately aligning the 2½" markings on both sides of the cutting guide and the 45° marking on the seam line. Cut remaining 2 sides of bias squares.

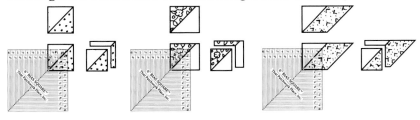

Vintage Fiesta Ware echoes the cheerful yellows found in the Handkerchief Basket quilt. Floral print handkerchiefs belonging to the author's grandmother were used in this quilt made for her mother. Quilted by Freda Smith.

4. Cut bias squares from the next row, working up the strip. Continue cutting bias squares until you have 7 for each basket.
5. Cut a triangle 6⅞" from each yellow print for Piece 2. It should measure 6⅞" along the 2 short sides.
6. Cut 1 square, 2⅞" x 2⅞", from each yellow print. Cut square once diagonally to yield 2 triangles for Piece 1.

From the white-on-white background fabric, cut:

    2 squares, each 10½" x 10½", for alternate blocks;

    12 rectangles, each 2½" x 6½", for Piece 3;

    6 squares, each 4⅞" x 4⅞". Cut squares once diagonally to yield 12 triangles for Piece 4.

From floral print, cut:
    2 squares, each 15½" x 15½". Cut squares twice diagonally to make 8 side
        setting triangles. You will only need 6.
    2 squares, each 8" x 8". Cut squares once diagonally to make 4 corner
        setting triangles.
From the yellow border fabric, cut:
    2 strips, each 2½" x 43", for side borders;
    2 strips, each 2½" x 33", for top and bottom borders.
From each handkerchief, cut:
    1 triangle, measuring 6⅞" along the 2 short sides for Piece 2.

DIRECTIONS

1. Piece 6 Basket blocks, using bias squares and the pieces cut from background and yellow prints.
2. Assemble blocks, alternate blocks, and side setting triangles into diagonal rows to form quilt top.
3. Add corner setting triangles.
4. Stitch borders to sides, then to top and bottom of quilt top.
5. Layer with batting and backing, then quilt or tie.
6. Bind with bias strips of fabric.

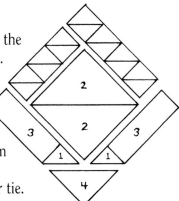

Quilting Suggestion: Quilt in the ditch to outline the upper basket triangles. Quilt ½" inside the seam for the lower basket. Quilt an intricate heart design* in the alternate blocks. Use a clamshell design for the handkerchief centers and in the border. You might want to quilt a special message in each heart. Echo quilt inside the side and corner setting triangles.

*Feathered heart design from *The Finishing Touch* by Shirley Thompson (Edmonds, Wash.: Powell Publications, 1980), p. 53.

Dresden Plate

Dimensions: 81" x 81"

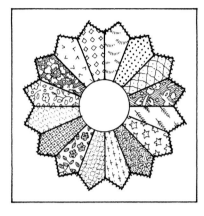

Dresden Plate block, 16"

Fabric Selection: Pastel colors were most commonly used for this pattern, which became popular in the 1930s. Select 12–16 pastel prints and a coordinating print for the border. Scraps from childhood dresses can also be utilized, making this a real "memory" quilt.

Materials: 44"-wide fabric

    4 yds. muslin or light-colored fabric for background, block centers, and binding

    ¼ yd. each of 12–16 pastel prints

    2⅜ yds. print for borders and sashing

    Blue or pink embroidery floss for decorative herringbone stitch

    4¾ yds. fabric for backing

    Batting and thread to finish

DIRECTIONS

1. Cut 16 squares of fabric, each 16½" x 16½", for background. Fold into quarters and crease lightly to aid in placement of appliqué, then open flat.
2. Using templates found on page 29, cut and piece 16 Dresden Plate blocks:
   a. Stitch plate segments (Template #2) together along straight edges.

An old Dresden Plate quilt covers a garden table set for an outdoor tea. Dresden china cups and plates will hold the tea cakes, home-made jam, and Cream-Cheese Foldovers (recipe on page 59).

b. Make a stiffened pressing template. Fold outer edges of segments over template and press in place.

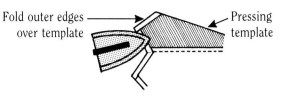

Fold outer edges over template — Pressing template

c. Center and baste a completed "plate" to each background block.

d. Using paper-patch appliqué technique on page 56, appliqué center circle cut from Template #1 over plate segments.

e. Secure edges of Dresden Plate, using the herringbone stitch.

Herringbone stitch

3. From the lengthwise grain of fabric, cut and set aside:
   2 strips, each 3¾" x 74½", for side borders;
   2 strips, each 3¾" x 81", for top and bottom borders.

4. Cut 12 sashing strips, each 4" x 16½", and 3 sashing strips, each 4" x 74½".

5. Join 4 blocks and 3 short sashing strips into a row. Make 4 of these rows.

6. Alternate rows of blocks and longer sashing strips. Stitch to form quilt top.

7. Stitch borders to sides, then add top and bottom borders.

8. Layer with batting and backing, then quilt or tie.

9. Bind with bias strips of fabric.

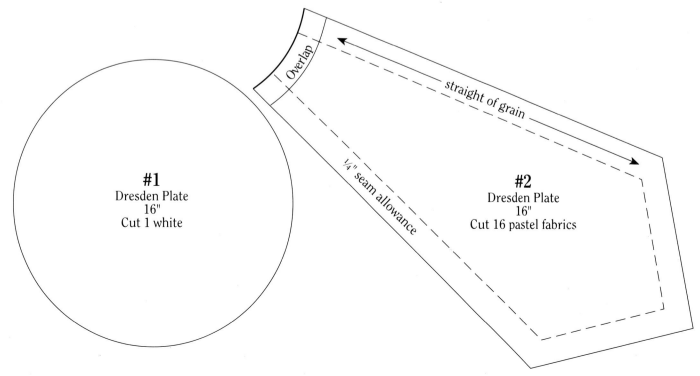

Quilting Suggestion: Quilt down the center of each segment and then "in the ditch" around outer edge of each block, between segments, and around center circle. Quilt a 1" grid in the background of each block. Use a simple cable design in the sashing and borders.

#1
Dresden Plate
16"
Cut 1 white

Overlap

straight of grain

¼" seam allowance

#2
Dresden Plate
16"
Cut 16 pastel fabrics

Dimensions: 66½" x 90"

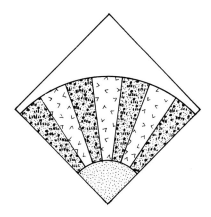

Fan block, 8"

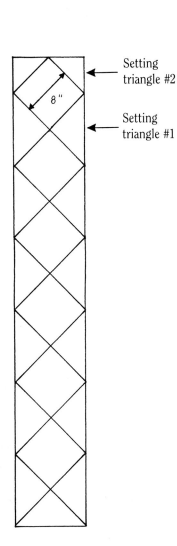

Setting triangle #2

8"

Setting triangle #1

Fabric Selection: Fans were quite popular with Victorian women and were often used by clever young ladies to send flirtatious messages to would-be suitors. A decorator fabric, featuring a ribbon and floral stripe, was selected for the vertical sashing strips of this very feminine quilt. A floral companion print was used for the setting triangles. Pastel colors for the fan segments and bows repeat the colors of the floral stripes and print, sending a romantic message.

Materials: 44"-wide fabric
- 1¼ yds. assorted light prints for background
- 3 yds. assorted pastel prints for fans and appliqué bows
- 2¼ yds. floral ribbon print for vertical strips and border (Print must have 6 repeats across fabric width, each approximately 8½" wide.)
- 1½ yds. large-scale, light-background print for setting triangles and binding
- 5¼ yds. fabric for backing
- Batting and thread to finish

DIRECTIONS

1. Cut 18 squares, each 8½" x 8½", from light prints for background. Using the templates on page 33, cut, piece, and appliqué 18 Fan blocks, using 2 pastel prints for each fan. (See paper-patch appliqué directions on page 56.) Alternate the fan segments so the deeper- or darker-colored segments are at the outside edges in each completed fan.

Stitch fan segments together

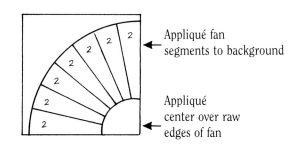

Appliqué fan segments to background

Appliqué center over raw edges of fan

2. From the large-scale print, cut:
   10 squares, each 12⅝" x 12⅝", for Setting Triangle #1. Cut squares twice diagonally to yield 40 triangles. You will need 39 of these.
   3 squares, each 6⅝" x 6⅝", for Setting Triangle #2. Cut squares once diagonally to yield 6 triangles.
3. Assemble 3 vertical strips, using 6 Fan blocks, 13 Setting Triangle #1, and 2 Setting Triangle #2 in each strip.

A floral-and-ribbon motif prevails in this Fantastic Fans strippy quilt by Judy Pollard of Seattle, Washington, and the Ribbons and Strawberries tea set. Serve the Strawberry Delight Cake (recipe on page 61) for an elegant afternoon tea.

4. Appliqué bows below fans, using paper-patch appliqué directions on page 56.

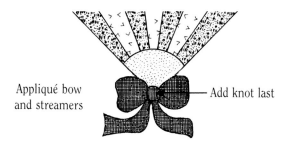

Appliqué bow
and streamers

Add knot last

5. Cut 4 lengthwise strips from floral ribbon fabric, each 8½" x 74".
6. Stitch vertical fan strips between the strips of floral ribbon fabric to form quilt top.

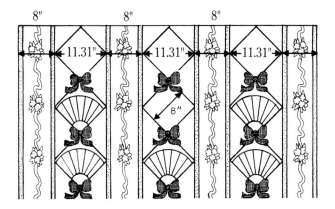

7. Cut top and bottom borders from floral ribbon fabric, each 8½" x 66½". Stitch to quilt top.
8. Layer with batting and backing, then quilt or tie.
9. Bind with bias strips of fabric.

Quilting Suggestion: Outline quilt around fan segments, fan center, bow, and streamers. Select a major design element in the strips of the floral ribbon fabric, such as a vine or ribbon streamer, and outline that element as it repeats across the quilt top. Quilt "in the ditch" around edges of blocks, set pieces, and vertical fabric segments.

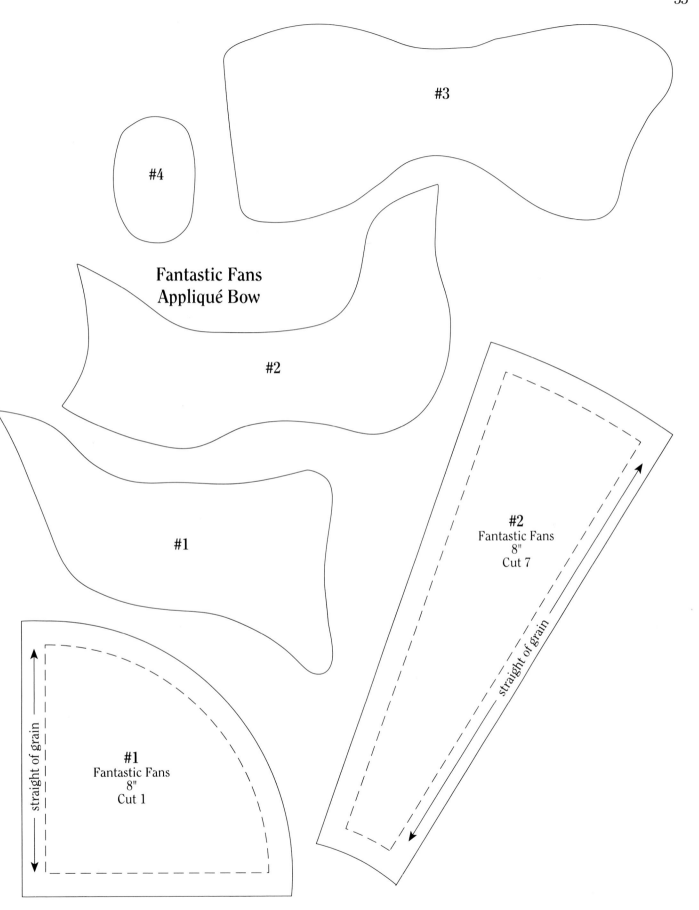

#3

#4

Fantastic Fans
Appliqué Bow

#2

#1

#2
Fantastic Fans
8"
Cut 7

straight of grain

#1
Fantastic Fans
8"
Cut 1

straight of grain

Molly, Kirsten, and Samantha, the three character dolls from Pleasant Company, are dressed in their summer outfits for afternoon tea. Both the dolls and the little girls whom the author invites from her neighborhood enjoy the Chocolate-Covered Strawberries (recipe on page 63). Behind the dolls' tea set is a wonderful doll quilt: Fan Tan Fantasy by Judy Pollard of Seattle, Washington.

A Doll's Tea Party

Dimensions: 21½" x 21½"

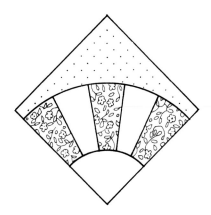

Fan block, 2¾"

Fabric Selection: A chintz floral fabric used for the broderie perse flowers in this quilt was selected as the theme fabric. A coordinating large-scale print in soft colors was chosen for the setting triangles. The pastel tones found in the flowers were repeated in the small Fan blocks, while a small-scale stripe works well for the vertical sashing.

Materials: 44"-wide fabric
- ½ yd. light print for fan background
- 1 yd. assorted pastel prints for fans
- 1 yd. large-scale, pastel print for setting triangles and border
- ⅝ yd. striped fabric for setting strips and inner border
- ¼ yd. print for binding
- ¼ yd. floral chintz for appliqué cutouts
- 2 yds. ¼"-wide ribbon
- ¾ yd. fabric for backing
- Embroidery floss to match ribbon
- Batting and thread to finish

Directions

Stitch fan segments together

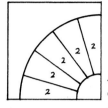

Appliqué fan segments to background

Appliqué center over raw edges of fan

1. Cut 12 squares, each 3¼" x 3¼", from background fabric. Using the templates on page 36, cut, piece, and appliqué 12 Fan blocks.
2. From large-scale print, cut:
   2 strips, each 3" x 17¼", for side borders;
   2 strips, each 3" x 22½", for top and bottom borders.
3. From remaining large-scale print, cut:
   6 squares, each 2⅞" x 2⅞", for Setting Triangle #2. Cut squares once diagonally to yield 12 triangles.
   5 squares, each 5⅛" x 5⅛", for Setting Triangle #1. Cut squares twice diagonally to yield 20 triangles. You will need only 18.
4. Assemble 3 vertical strips, using 4 Fan blocks, 6 Setting Triangle #1, and 4 Setting Triangle #2 in each strip.
5. Cut 2 strips, each 2¼" x 16", from striped fabric.
6. Stitch striped-fabric strips between the vertical fan strips to form quilt top.

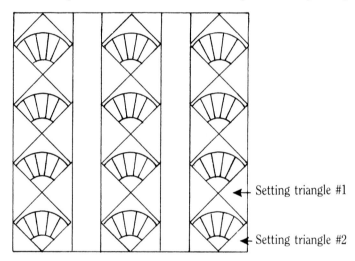

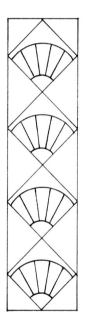

← Setting triangle #1

← Setting triangle #2

7. From colored stripe, cut:
   2 strips, each ⅞" x 16", for side borders;
   2 strips, each ⅞" x 16⅜", for top and bottom borders.
8. Stitch inner borders to sides, then to top and bottom of quilt top. Add outer borders to sides, then to top and bottom.
9. Cut flowers from chintz fabric. Randomly place on setting strips and in 3 corners, utilizing floral design shapes to their best advantage. Appliqué in place, following directions for paper-patch appliqué on page 56.

Appliqué chintz flower cutouts

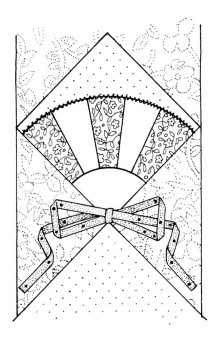

10. Embroider a herringbone stitch along the top edge of the second fan in the right fan strip.

11. Layer with batting and backing, then quilt or tie.
12. Cut an 18" length of ribbon. Tie into a bow with long streamers. Position on fan with herringbone stitching. Tack in place and then secure by stitching French knots along the bow and streamers.
13. Tie remaining ribbon into a bow with very long streamers. Tack in place below floral appliqué in upper left corner. Secure by stitching French knots along the bow and streamers.
14. Bind with bias strips of fabric.

Quilting Suggestion: Quilt "in the ditch" around fan segments and block outlines. Quilt diagonal lines, ¼" apart, reversing direction of the lines above the fans and in the set pieces. Quilt along stripes in strips between Fan blocks. Quilt around chintz flower appliqués. For border, quilt lines ½" apart, echoing corner shape. Interrupt these lines with diagonal lines spaced ½" apart near the center of each border.

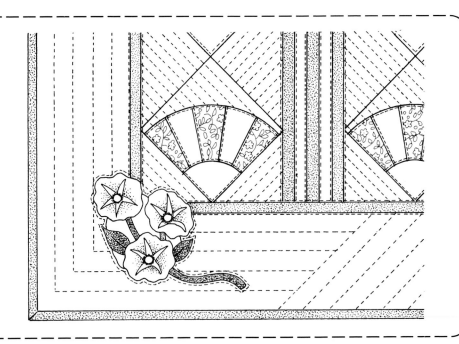

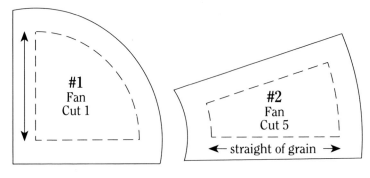

#1
Fan
Cut 1

#2
Fan
Cut 5

← straight of grain →

Fabric Selection: These floral felines with their three-dimensional tails have settled down for a cat nap after a refreshing bit of catnip tea. The cats are appliquéd to pastel woven plaid or striped handkerchiefs, usually sold in packages of twelve. You may utilize large-scale floral scraps from decorating projects for the cat bodies. A multi-striped fabric is used for the outer border, while its companion fabric is used for the sashing and binding. Embroidered faces and perky bows add the finishing touches.

Materials: 44"-wide fabric

- 12 woven pastel plaid or striped handkerchiefs at least 10" square for block background
- ¼ yd. each of 12 different floral fabrics for cats
- 5 yds. total of assorted pastel ribbon
- 1½ yds. multi-striped fabric for borders (Fabric must have at least 4 repeats across width.)
- 1¼ yds. companion print for sashing and binding
- 1½ yds. fabric for backing
- Pink and blue embroidery floss for faces
- Batting and thread to finish

Dimensions: 36½" x 46½"

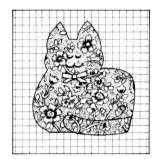

Cat block, 9"

The Catnip Tea quilt features wonderful floral felines who would love a bit of catnip tea and jam tarts served from the Russian tea set. Pastel woven handkerchiefs serve as the background for the appliquéd cats. Quilted by Beverly Payne.

DIRECTIONS

1. Trim handkerchiefs to 9½" x 9½". These will be the background for the appliqué.

2. Using the cat template on page 40 and following the paper-patch appliqué directions on page 56, cut cats from floral fabric, prepare, and stitch one to each background square.

3. Fold a leftover piece of each floral fabric with right sides together and trace pattern piece for tail onto wrong side of fabric. Sew pieces together, stitching directly on the drawn line and leaving an opening along the straight edge for turning. Cut away excess fabric ⅛" from stitching line. Clip curves. Turn to right side.

Trace pattern piece with pencil

4. Using pink or blue embroidery floss, stitch cat face and/or whiskers.

5. Stitch tail to each appliquéd cat along placement line as shown. Tail may be lightly stuffed for added dimension, if desired. Tack in place.

Stitch tail here then fold to cover raw edge

6. Cut 9 strips of fabric, each 1½" x 9½", for horizontal sashing. Join 4 Cat blocks and 3 sashing strips into vertical rows.

7. Cut 2 vertical sashing strips, each 1½" x 39½". Join vertical rows of blocks with sashing strips.

8. From the striped fabric, cut borders, paying careful attention to the multi-striped pattern and its placement. Cut:
   2 strips, each 4" x 50", for side borders;
   2 strips, each 4" x 40", for top and bottom borders.

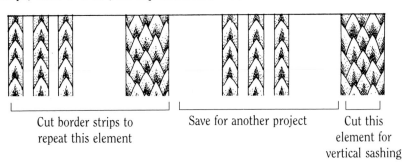

Cut border strips to repeat this element   Save for another project   Cut this element for vertical sashing

Quilt back

9. To attach borders with mitered corners:
   a. Center and stitch a border strip to each edge of the quilt top so that the strip extends an equal distance beyond each end of the quilt. Stitch, using a ¼"-wide seam allowance, beginning and ending ¼" from each edge of the quilt. Backstitch at both ends.

b. Using a ruler with a 45° marking, mark the wrong side of each strip. Mark a line from corner of stitching line to the intersection of border strips.

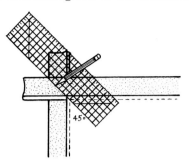

c. Pin carefully, matching markings. Stitch along marked line, backstitching at both ends.

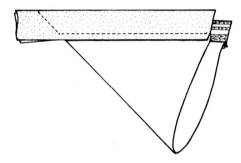

d. Trim seams to ¼" and press open.

10. Layer with batting and backing, then quilt or tie.

11. Bind with bias strips of fabric

12. Cut ribbon into twelve 15" lengths. Place ribbon under cat face and bartack in place by hand or machine. Tie each ribbon into a bow. Trim ends, if necessary.

Quilting Suggestion: Outline quilt ½" inside each cat shape. Quilt a diagonal grid through the handkerchief background. Quilt "in the ditch" along sashing. Select several of the stripes in the border and quilt alongside their edges.

40

Catnip Tea Appliqué
and Tail Templates

X
Tack tail here

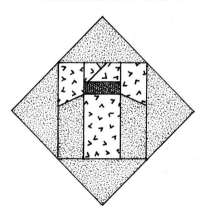

The Japanese Tea Ceremony quilt, designed by Merlin Sampson of New Zealand, features the Kimono block. A Japanese tea set is used to serve the green tea and rice crackers. Quilted by Freda Smith.

Japanese Tea Ceremony

Fabric Selection: Thirteen small geometric, black-and-white prints, reminiscent of Japanese fabrics, were selected for the kimonos. A bold black-and-white print was used for the setting triangles. The red print border repeats the red used for the kimono sash (obi).

Materials: 44"-wide fabric
- ¼ yd. each of 13 black-and-white prints for kimonos
- ½ yd. solid black for block background and binding
- ¼ yd. red solid for sashes
- ½ yd. black-and-white print for setting triangles
- ⅜ yd. red print for borders (cut crosswise)
- ⅞ yd. print or solid for backing
- Batting and thread to finish

Dimensions: 29¼" x 29¼"

Kimono block, 5½"

DIRECTIONS

1. Using the templates on page 42, cut and piece 13 Kimono blocks.

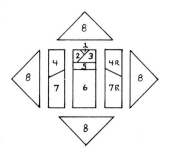

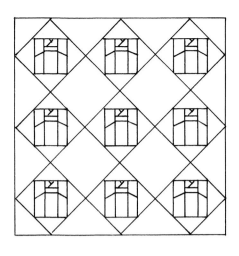

2. Cut the following setting triangles from black-and-white prints:
   2 squares, each 9¼" x 9¼", for side setting triangles. Cut squares twice diagonally to yield 8 triangles.
   2 squares, each 4¾" x 4¾", for corner setting triangles. Cut squares once diagonally to yield 4 triangles.
3. Join Kimono blocks and setting triangles into diagonal rows. Then, join rows to form quilt top.
4. From the red print fabric, cut:
   2 strips, each 3¼" x 23¾", for side borders;
   2 strips, each 3¼" x 29¼", for top and bottom borders.
5. Stitch borders to sides, then to top and bottom of quilt top.
6. Layer with batting and backing, then quilt or tie.
7. Bind with bias strips of fabric.

Quilting Suggestion: Outline quilt around each kimono, then quilt "in the ditch" around the edge of each block. Quilt diagonal lines in each border, radiating from the center.

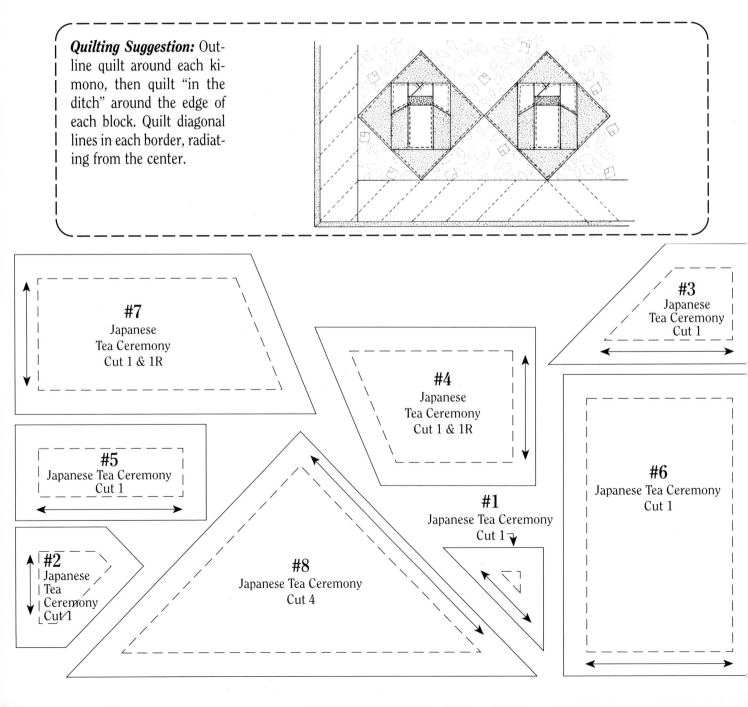

#7
Japanese
Tea Ceremony
Cut 1 & 1R

#3
Japanese
Tea Ceremony
Cut 1

#4
Japanese
Tea Ceremony
Cut 1 & 1R

#5
Japanese Tea Ceremony
Cut 1

#6
Japanese Tea Ceremony
Cut 1

#2
Japanese
Tea
Ceremony
Cut 1

#8
Japanese Tea Ceremony
Cut 4

#1
Japanese Tea Ceremony
Cut 1

Dimensions: 77½" x 77½"

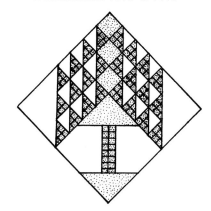

Pine Tree block, 14"

Fabric Selection: Twelve different plaid fabrics are used for the Pine Tree blocks. Select flannel shirt plaids to create a rugged, outdoorsy look, or use plaid scraps from old school dresses for a Christmas quilt full of memories. Red or green center squares highlight each Pine Tree block, while a strong red-and-green plaid is used for the sashing squares and borders. Template-Free™ cutting and piecing make this quilt a snap to make, allowing time for the hand-appliquéd holly leaves.

Materials: 44"-wide fabric
    4 yds. light fabric for background
    ½ yd. each of 12 plaid fabrics (or 12 fat quarters) for trees
    1 yd. assorted red and green fabrics for contrasting squares and
        triangles, holly leaves, and berries
    ⅜ yd. red print for inner border (cut crosswise)
    1½ yds. plaid fabric for outer borders and sashing squares
    4½ yds. fabric for backing
    Batting, binding, and thread to finish

TEMPLATE-FREE™ CUTTING:

From the plaid fabric (for the outer border and sashing squares), cut:
    9 squares, each 2½" x 2½", for sashing squares;
    2 strips, each 5½" x 67½", for side borders;
    2 strips, each 5½" x 77½", for top and bottom borders.
From the plaid fabrics for trees and the background fabric, make bias squares for the Pine Tree blocks. You will need 24 bias squares for each block.

1. Cut 3 bias strips, 2½" wide, from each plaid. Cut 2 pieces, each ½-yard long, from the background fabric. From this, cut 24 strips, 2½" wide. For each Pine Tree block, alternate the plaid and background fabric strips, beginning and ending with the plaid fabric. Stitch strips with right sides together, using a ¼"-wide seam. Press seams toward plaid fabric.

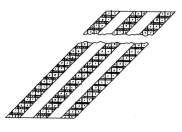

2. Beginning at lower end of strips, cut the first 2 sides of the bias squares, aligning the 45° marking on the seam line.

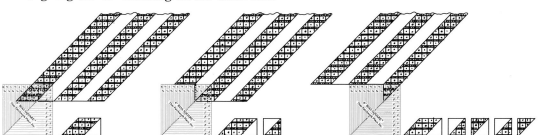

3. Turn cut segments and place Bias Square® on the opposite 2 sides, accurately aligning the 2½" markings on both sides of the cutting guide and the 45° marking on the seam line. Cut remaining 2 sides of bias squares.

A Christmas tea is served on Cuthbertson Christmas Tree china, which repeat the fabric used in Plaid Pines. An elegant Buche de Noel (traditional Christmas yule log dessert, recipe on page 61) highlights the holiday season. Quilted by Marta Estes.

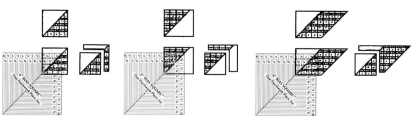

4. Cut bias squares from the next row, working up the strip. Continue cutting bias squares until you have 18 bias squares.

5. Resize the edge triangles, using the template provided on page 46 for Piece 2. You will need 6 for each block.

6. Cut a tree trunk, 1½" x 6", from each piece of plaid fabric for Piece 6. From the background fabric, cut:

12 squares, each 6⅞" x 6⅞". Cut squares once diagonally to make 24 triangles for Piece 4.

24 strips, each 2½" x 14½", for sashing;

1 square, 21" x 21". Cut square twice diagonally to make 4 side setting triangles.

2 squares, each 22⅛" x 22⅛". Cut square once diagonally to make 4 corner triangles.

12 and 12R pieces of background fabric from Template #1 on page 46 for the Pine Tree block.

From the assorted red and green fabrics, choose a fabric to contrast with the bias squares in each block. For example, if the bias squares in the block contain green half-square triangles, choose red (and vice versa). Cut:

3 squares, each 2½" x 2½", for Piece 3;

1 square, 5" x 5". Cut square once diagonally for Piece 5.

From the red fabric for the inner border, cut:

2 strips, each 65½" x 1½", for side borders;

2 strips, each 67½" x 1½", for top and bottom borders.

From the assorted green fabrics, cut:

12 holly leaves for appliqué, using the template provided on page 46. Prepare for appliqué, following paper-patch appliqué directions on page 56.

From the assorted red fabrics, cut:

12 holly berries, using the templates provided on page 46. Prepare for appliqué, following the paper-patch appliqué directions on page 56.

DIRECTIONS

1. Piece 12 Pine Tree blocks, using background, bias squares, and contrasting red and green fabrics.

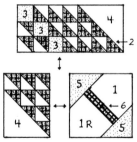

2. Join Pine Tree blocks with sashing strips and side setting triangles into diagonal rows. Join sashing strips and squares into rows. Join together in a diagonal setting. Trim away excess sashing strips along edges.

3. Add corner triangles cut from background fabric to quilt top. Appliqué holly leaves and berries to corner triangles, following paper-patch appliqué directions on page 56.

4. Stitch inner borders to sides, then add top and bottom inner borders.

5. Stitch outer borders to sides. Add top and bottom outer borders.

6. Layer with batting and backing, then quilt or tie.

7. Bind with bias strips of fabric.

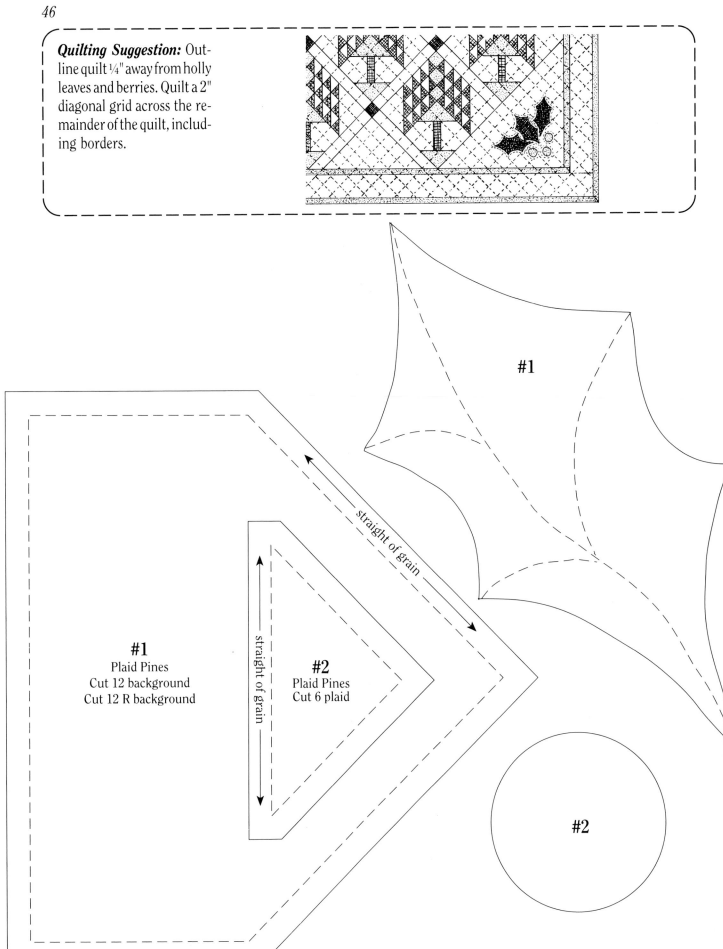

Quilting Suggestion: Outline quilt ¼" away from holly leaves and berries. Quilt a 2" diagonal grid across the remainder of the quilt, including borders.

straight of grain

#1

#1
Plaid Pines
Cut 12 background
Cut 12 R background

straight of grain

#2
Plaid Pines
Cut 6 plaid

#2

Special Projects: Kitchen Cats

This delightful cat pillow can easily be turned into a doorstop by inserting a brick or other heavy object inside the cat body.

Finished Size: 11" tall

Materials

1 linen dish towel, approximately 18" x 26"
¾ yd. ½"-wide ribbon
Polyester fiberfill stuffing

DIRECTIONS

1. Fold linen dish towel in half with right sides together. Using pattern piece on pages 48–49, cut 2 cat bodies.
2. Stitch around outside edges, using a ¼"-wide seam. Reinforce stitching at sharp curve of neck and tail with a second row of stitching. Clip curves and turn right side out.
3. Stuff cat loosely with fiberfill stuffing. Slipstitch opening closed.
4. Tie ribbon around cat's neck and into a bow.

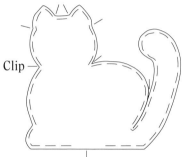

Perky house cats made from woven linen dish towels rest amidst hand-painted house dishes. Serve shortbread or Langue de Chat (Cat's Tongue) cookies (recipe on page 63) and homemade jam.

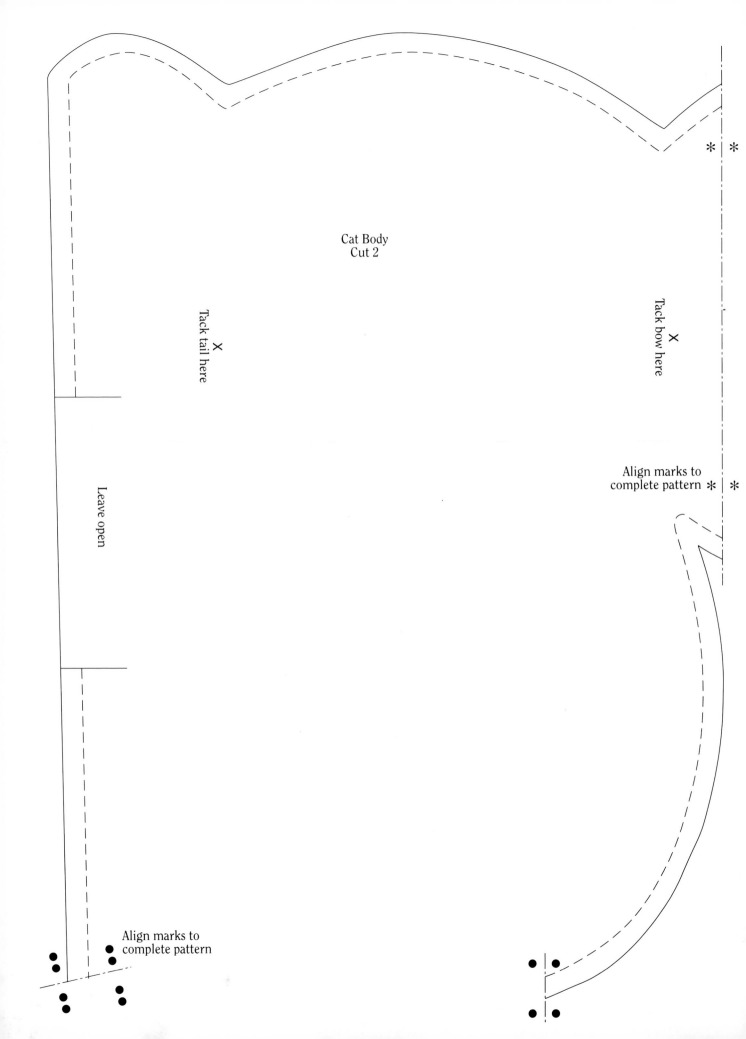

Cat Body
Cut 2

Tack tail here
X

Tack bow here
X

Leave open

Align marks to
complete pattern

Align marks to
complete pattern ∗ | ∗

∗ | ∗

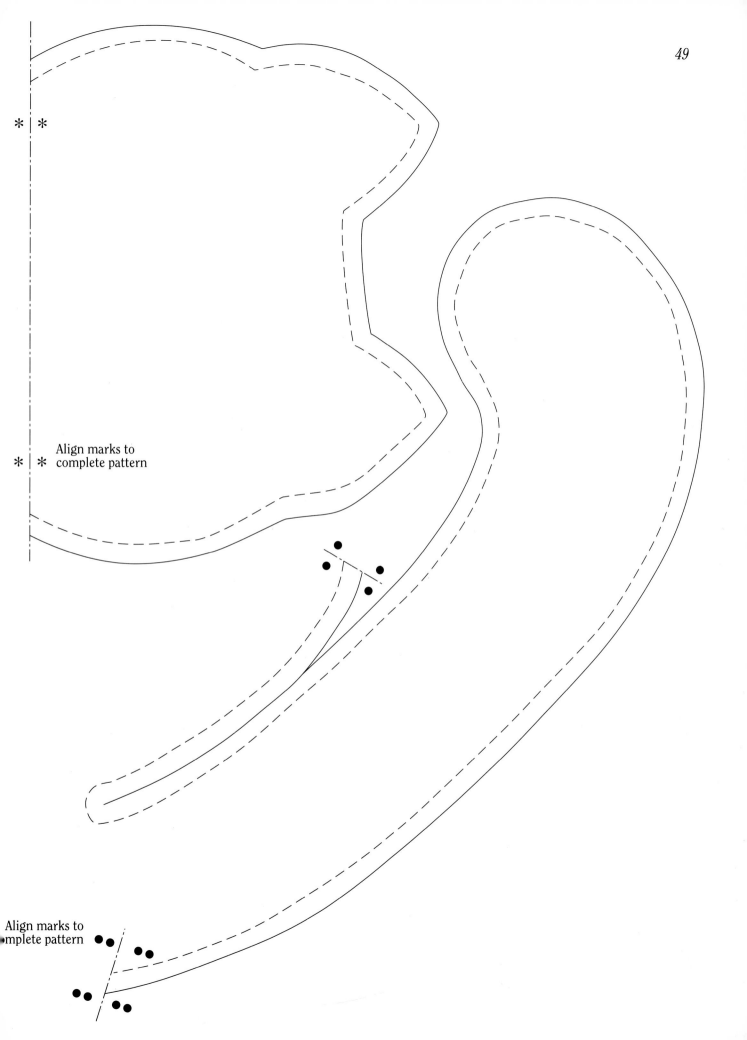

* | *

* | * Align marks to
complete pattern

Align marks to
mplete pattern

The Bridal Pillow utilizes a legacy of family stitches: Grandmother's crocheted doilies and lace edging, a floral handkerchief from the 1930s, Aunt Minnie's embroidery work, and Aunt Bea's cross-stitch. Mother's lace wedding glove adds a special touch. Embroider the wedding date and the couple's initials near the two hearts. Fresh strawberries with a Sour Cream Dip (recipe on page 63) accompany tea served from a Berries and Cream tea set.

Bridal Pillow

Finished Size: 21" x 30½"

Materials: 44"-wide fabric

1 yd. pastel moiré print for background
Assorted doilies, laces, handkerchiefs, and trims for embellishment
2 yds. ⅛"-wide ribbon
3 yds. 2"-wide lace trim (or utilize crocheted trim from old linens)
1 yd. muslin for pillow form
Polyester fiberfill stuffing

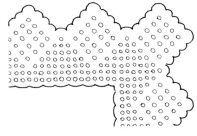

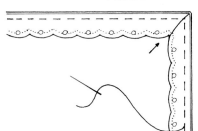

DIRECTIONS

1. Cut 2 rectangles from background fabric, each 21½" x 31", or size appropriate to your crocheted lace trim. Set 1 rectangle aside to use as the pillow back.
2. Following the directions on page 10, cover the remaining rectangle with lace collage.
3. Add embroidery embellishments and button clusters as desired. See pages 7–9 for suggestions.
4. Baste lace or crocheted trim around outside edges, placing scalloped edge toward center of pillow. Allow extra lace at corners if you are not using a crocheted edging with turned corners.
5. Pin pillow front to pillow back, right sides together. Stitch, using a ¼"-wide seam allowance and leaving an opening for turning and inserting pillow form or stuffing. Turn right side out. Insert pillow form and hand sew closed

Tea Cozy

Materials: 44"-wide fabric

Finished Size: 14" x 16"

Cover: ½ yd. fabric for background
Assorted doilies, laces, buttons, and trims for embellishment
1¼ yds. narrow lace trim
⅛ yd. 1"-wide ribbon
½ yd. coordinating fabric for lining
½ yd. thin batting

Pad: 1 yd. muslin
½ yd. extra-thick batting

DIRECTIONS

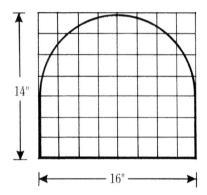

1. To make the Tea Cozy, you will need 2 large templates: the inner pad (A) and the tea cozy (B). On a large sheet of graph paper (17½" x 22" is best), measure a 14" x 16" grid of 2" squares. Study the illustration provided. It shows the shape for the pad, Template A. Copy the pad shape, square by square, onto the larger grid. Make Template B, the tea-cozy shape, by duplicating the pad shape and adding a ½"-wide seam allowance all the way around.

2. Cut two 16" x 18" rectangles from the background fabric. Lightly trace the tea-cozy shape (Template B) onto the rectangles, but do not cut them out at this time.

3. Cover both pieces of background fabric with lace collage, following the directions on page 10.

4. Place Template B on top of each piece of background fabric and cut to the appropriate shape and size.

5. Using Template B, cut 2 from the lining and 2 from the thin batting. Layer batting and lining behind each of the lace-embellished tea-cozy pieces. Baste each together around curved edge.

6. Baste lace trim to curved edge of one tea-cozy piece, placing straight edge on the ½" seam line and the scalloped edge toward the center.

Baste lace trim

7. Fold ribbon in half, center, and pin to top of tea cozy, placing raw edges even with tea-cozy edge.

Raw edges of ribbon

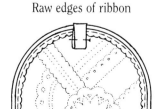

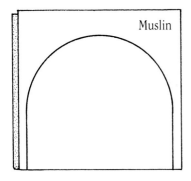

Muslin

8. With right sides together, stitch tea-cozy sections together, using a ½"-wide seam allowance, catching ribbon and trim in seam.

9. Turn tea cozy right side out. The raw edges of the seam will be hidden by the inner pad.

10. Cut a 2½" x 34" strip of fabric. Use to bind lower edges of tea cozy, following binding directions on page 58.

11. Make the removable pad for the tea cozy:

    a. Cut 2 pieces of unbleached muslin, each 18" x 36", and 2 pieces of thick batting or several layers of thin batting, each 18" x 18".

    b. Fold the muslin rectangles in half, as shown, and press in creases. With muslin pieces still folded, place Template A (pad shape) with the bottom of the template on the crease and trace the curved outline onto the fabric with a fabric marking pen. Mark only one side of each folded piece.

    c. Unfold the muslin pieces with the marked side down. Place the batting with bottom edge along the crease in the muslin. Fold the muslin back to cover the batting. Pin baste through all 3 layers along the marked outline.

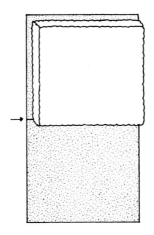
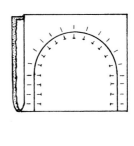

    d. With a straight machine stitch, stitch through the 3 layers ¼" inside the curved line. Make a second line of stitching on the line. After stitching the curves on each pad section, remove the pins from one pad and trim to ⅛" outside stitching. Do not trim the other pad.

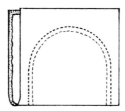
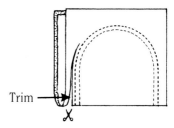

Trim

    e. Carefully pin baste the trimmed pad to the untrimmed pad, matching the sewn curves. Keep the trimmed pad on top. Stitch the pads together with a straight stitch along the curve that falls between the 2 previous rows of stitching.

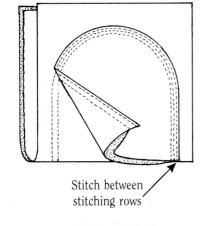

Stitch between stitching rows

f. Remove pins and trim away remaining excess muslin and batting, being careful not to cut the stitches. The resulting raw edge will remain on the outside of the pad and be hidden by the decorative cover.

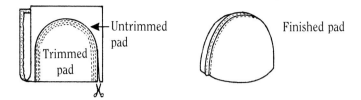

12. Insert pad into tea cozy. Wash the pad and tea cozy separately by hand or in the machine at a gentle setting.

This romantic tea cozy embellished with lace collage is almost too pretty to be used over the sewing-machine teapot. I learned to enjoy Lemon Honey (recipe on page 59) on scones while taking tea with my hostess at a New Zealand sheep station.

Glossary of Techniques

MACHINE PIECING

For machine piecing, use white or neutral thread as light in color as the lightest fabric in the project. Use a dark neutral thread for piecing dark solids. It is easier to work with 100% cotton thread on some machines. Check your needle. If it is dull, burred, or bent, replace it with a new one.

Sew exact ¼" seams. To determine the ¼" seam allowance on your machine, place a template under the presser foot and gently lower the needle onto the seam line. The distance from the needle to the edge of the template is ¼". Lay a piece of masking tape at the edge of the template to act as a guide. Stitch length should be set at 10–12 stitches per inch. For most of the sewing in this book, sew from cut edge to cut edge (exceptions will be noted). Backtack, if you wish, although it is really not necessary, as each seam will be crossed and held by another.

Press the seam allowances to one side, toward the darker fabric when possible. Avoid too much pressing as you sew because it tends to stretch bias edges and distorts fabric shapes.

To piece a block, sew the smallest pieces together first to form units. Join smaller units to form larger ones until the block is complete.

Seams need not be pinned unless matching is involved, or the seam is longer than 4". Keep pins away from the seam line. Sewing over pins tends to burr the needle and makes it hard to be accurate in tight places.

Here are six matching techniques that can be helpful in many different piecing situations.

Opposing Seams: When stitching one seamed unit to another, press seam allowances on the seams that need to match in opposite directions. The two "opposing" seams will hold each other in place and evenly distribute the bulk. Plan pressing to take advantage of opposing seams.

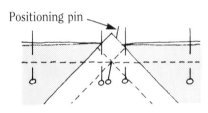

Positioning Pin: A pin, carefully pushed straight through two points that need to match and pulled tight, will establish the proper point of matching. Pin the seam normally and remove the positioning pin before stitching.

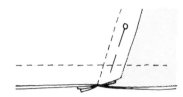

The X: When triangles are pieced, stitches will form an X at the next seam line. Stitch through the center of the X to make sure the points on the sewn triangles will not be chopped off.

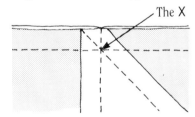

Easing: When two pieces sewn together are supposed to match but instead are slightly different lengths, pin the points of matching and stitch with the shorter piece on top. The feed dog will help ease the fullness of the bottom piece.

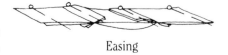

Easing

TEMPLATE-FREE™ TECHNIQUES

Special tools and Template-Free™ techniques speed the cutting and piecing process and ensure accuracy. For more information on Template-Free techniques, see *Shortcuts: A Concise Guide to Rotary Cutting* by Donna Thomas, published by That Patchwork Place.

TOOLS

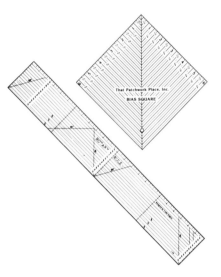

Rotary Cutter and Mat: A large rotary cutter will enable you to quickly cut strips and pieces without templates. A mat with a rough finish will hold the fabric in place and protect both the blade and the cutting table.

Cutting Guides: You will need a ruler for measuring and to guide the rotary cutter. The Rotary Rule™, made from ¼"-thick acrylic, includes markings for 45° and 60° angles, guidelines for use in crosscutting strips, plus the standard measurements. When you cut individual quilt pieces, a smaller guide, such as the Bias Square®, is helpful. The Bias Square is also required for cutting preassembled bias squares. The Rotary Rule™ and Bias Square® are available through That Patchwork Place, Inc., PO Box 118, Bothell, WA 98041.

All pieces are cut with the ¼" seam allowance included. If accurate ¼" seams are sewn by machine, there is no need to mark stitching lines.

WORKING WITH GRAIN LINES

Yarns are woven together to form fabric. It stretches or remains stable, depending on the grain line you are using. Lengthwise grain runs parallel to the selvage and has very little stretch. Crosswise grain runs from selvage to selvage and has some give to it. All other grains are considered bias. True bias is a grain that runs at a 45° angle to the lengthwise and crosswise grains.

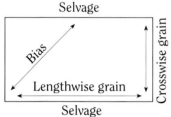

In most cases, the rotary-cutting directions have been written using the following guides for grain-line placement:

1. Squares and rectangles are cut on the lengthwise and crosswise grain of fabric.
2. Half-square triangles are cut with the short sides on the straight grain and the long side on the bias. Bias strip piecing produces sewn half-square triangles with grain lines that follow this guideline.
3. Quarter-square triangles have the short sides on the bias and the long side on the straight grain. They are generally used along the outside edges of the quilt, where the long edge will not stretch.
4. When you are working with striped fabric or special prints, the direction of the stripe or print takes precedence over the direction of the grain. Handle these pieces carefully, since they are not cut on the grain and will be less stable. If you are

going to use these pieces along the outside edges of the quilt, stay-stitch ⅛" from raw edge to avoid stretching.

TRIANGLES

Half-Square Triangles. These triangles are half of a square with the short sides on the straight grain of fabric and the long side on the bias. To cut these triangles, cut a square and then cut it in half diagonally. Cut the square ⅞" larger than the finished short side of the triangle to allow for all seam allowances.

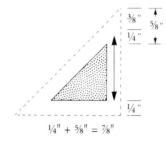

1. Cut a strip the desired finished measurement plus ⅞".
2. Cut into squares, using the same measurement.

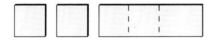

3. Cut a stack of squares diagonally, corner to corner.

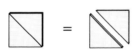

Quarter-Square Triangles. Triangles used along the outside edges of a quilt are quarter-square triangles. These triangles have their short sides on the bias and the long side on the straight grain. This makes them easier to handle and keeps the outside edges of your quilt from stretching. These triangles are cut from squares. Each square is cut 1¼" larger than the finished long side of the triangle.

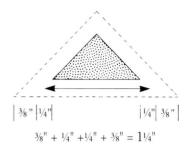

1. Cut a strip the desired finished measurement plus 1¼".
2. Cut into squares, using the same measurement.

3. Cut a stack of these squares (at least four) diagonally by lining up the ruler from corner to opposite corner. Without moving these pieces, cut in the other direction to make an X. Each square will yield four triangles with the long side on grain.

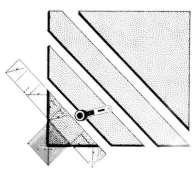

BIAS SQUARES

The Handkerchief Basket and Plaid Pines quilts contain squares from two contrasting triangles. The short sides of the triangles are on the straight grain of fabric while the long sides are on the bias. These are called bias-square units.

1. To make fabric more manageable, cut two half-yard or smaller pieces of contrasting fabric and layer with right sides facing up. The fabric strips will be cut at the same time.
2. Use the 45° marking on the cutting guide; use a longer ruler to make a bias cut.

3. Cut strips the same width as the bias square you are cutting. For example, cut bias strips 2½" wide for 2½" bias squares. After piecing, you will have 2" finished bias squares.

4. Sew the strips together on the long bias edge with ¼" seams. Press seams toward the dark fabric.

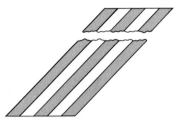

5. Align 45° marking on Bias Square® with seam line. Cut first two sides of square after measuring distance from cut edge to opposite side of square. Measure and cut third and fourth sides in the same manner.

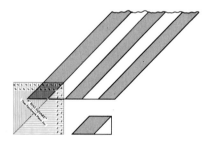

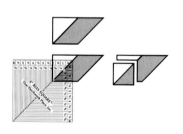

6. Align 45° marking on Bias Square with seam line before cutting the next bias square. Edge triangles will result along outer edges. These may be used in your quilt design by placing a template on the edge triangles and cutting them to the correct size.

7. All directions give cut size for bias squares; finished size will be ½" smaller.

Appliqué

Paper-Patch Appliqué

1. Make a stiffened template of each shape in the appliqué design. Do not add seam allowances to the templates.

2. On bond-weight paper, trace around the stiffened templates to make a paper patch for each shape in the appliqué design.

3. Pin each paper patch to the wrong side of the fabric.

4. Cut out fabric shapes, adding ¼" seam allowance all around each paper shape.

5. With your fingers, turn the seam allowance over the edge of the paper and baste to paper. Baste inside curves first (a little clipping may be necessary to help the fabric stretch). On outside curves, take small running stitches through fabric only to ease in fullness. Take an occasional stitch through the paper to hold fabric in place. Follow this basting order (inside curves first, outside curves last) when appliquéing the fabric piece to the block, easing fullness and bias stretch outward.

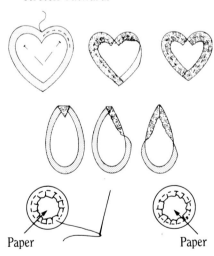

Paper   Paper

6. When all the seam allowances are turned and basted, press the appliqué pieces. Then, position and pin the pieces in place on the background fabric. Template numbers identify each appliqué piece and in-

dicate the order in which they are to be sewn. Be sure to appliqué each piece in the correct sequence or you will find yourself taking out stitches to tuck in other pieces.

7. Using a small, blind hemming stitch and a single matching thread (i.e., green thread for a green leaf), appliqué shapes to the background.

a. Start the first stitch from the back of the block. Bring the needle up through the background fabric and through the folded edge of the appliqué piece.

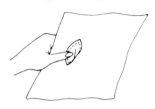

b. Insert the needle right next to where you brought it up, but this time put it through only the background fabric.

c. Bring the needle up through both layers of fabric, approximately ⅛" or less from the first stitch.

d. Space your stitches a little less than ⅛" apart.

Machine Appliqué

For machine appliqué, do not add seam allowances before cutting out pieces. Use a glue stick or Wonder-Under™, a fusible webbing, to hold pieces in position. Sew around each appliqué piece with a narrow, close zigzag stitch, using thread to match the appliqué fabric.

Fusible Appliqué

Wonder-Under™ has absolutely refined quick appliqués. It has a paper backing, on which you can trace before fusing it to the fabric. Trace all of the appliqué patterns needed, keeping in mind that you are tracing them in reverse. Leave room between patterns to cut them apart. Cut apart and, following manufacturer's directions, fuse them to the wrong side of desired fabrics. By doing this, you don't have to guess how much fabric you will need to cover. Cut out fabric appliqués on the drawn lines, remove the paper backing, and position appliqués on the background fabric. Again, follow manufacturer's directions for final fusing. At this point, you have several options. You can machine stitch the appliqués, you can work around the appliqués by hand with a buttonhole stitch, or you can leave the appliqués as they are. For a quick and simple wall hanging, fusing the appliqués is sufficient. The project cannot be washed and should be rolled up instead of folded to store, but, with minimum effort, you will have a decoration that can provide years of enjoyment.

DIAGONAL QUILT SETTINGS

Diagonally set quilts are made with blocks that are turned "on point" so that the straight of grain in each block runs diagonally. When this type of quilt is hung, it has a tendency to sag. To help control this tendency, cut the setting triangles that surround the blocks so that the straight of grain runs up and down, parallel to the long edge of the triangle. These triangles give support to the blocks and help stabilize them. However, when joining the blocks to the setting triangles, you will be joining a bias edge to a straight-of-grain edge, which can be tricky. If the bias cut edge is quite stretchy, you may want to staystitch in the seam allowance to stabilize.

Join blocks and setting triangles into diagonal rows. Then, join rows to form the quilt top.

PREPARING TO QUILT

MARKING

In most cases, before you quilt, the quilt top must be marked with lines to guide stitching. Where you place the quilting lines will depend on the patchwork design, the type of batting used, and how much quilting you want to do.

Try to avoid quilting too close to the seam lines, where the bulk of seam allowances might slow you down or make the stitches uneven. Also, keep in mind that the purpose of quilting, besides its aesthetic value, is to securely hold the three quilt layers together. Don't leave large areas unquilted.

Thoroughly press the quilt top and mark it before it is assembled with the batting and backing. You will need marking pencils, a long ruler or yardstick, stencils or templates for quilting motifs, and a large, clean, flat surface on which to work. Use a sharp marking pencil and lightly mark the quilting lines on the fabric.

BACKING

A single length of 45"-wide fabric can often be used for backing small quilts. To be safe, plan on a usable width of only 42" after shrinkage and cutting off selvages. For larger quilts, two lengths of fabric will have to be sewn together. Press seams open.

Cut the backing 1" larger than the quilt top all the way around. Press thoroughly. Lay the backing face down on your work surface. With masking tape, tape the backing down (without stretching) to keep it smooth and flat while working with the other layers.

BATTING

Batting is the filler in a quilt or comforter. Thick batting is used with comforters that are tied. If you plan to quilt, use thin batting and quilt by hand.

Thin batting comes in 100% cotton, 100% polyester, and a cotton-polyester (80%–20%) combination. All cotton batting requires close quilting to prevent shifting and separating in the wash. Most old quilts have cotton batting and are rather flat. Cotton is a good natural fiber that lasts well and is compatible with cotton and cotton-blend fabrics. Less quilting is required with 100% polyester batting. If polyester batting is glazed or bonded, it is easy to handle, won't pull apart, and has more loft than cotton batting.

ASSEMBLING THE LAYERS

Center the freshly ironed and marked quilt top on top of the batting, face up. Starting in the middle, pin baste the three layers together while gently smoothing out fullness to the sides and corners. Take care not to distort the straight lines of the quilt design and the borders.

After pinning, baste the layers together with needle and light-colored thread. Start in the middle and make a line of large stitches to each corner to form a large **X**. Continue basting in a grid of parallel lines 6"–8" apart. Finish with a row of basting around the outside edges. Quilts that will be quilted with a hoop or on your lap will require basting because they will be handled more than those quilted on a frame.

After basting, remove the pins. Now you are ready to quilt.

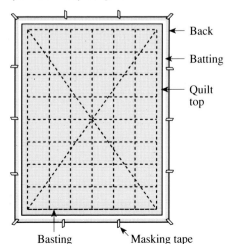

Back

Batting

Quilt top

Basting   Masking tape

HAND QUILTING

To quilt by hand, you will need quilting thread, quilting needles, small scissors, a thimble, and perhaps a balloon or a large rubber band to help grasp the needle if it gets stuck. Quilt on a frame, a large hoop, or just on your lap or a table. Use a single strand of quilting thread not longer than 18". Make a small single knot in the end of the thread. The quilting stitch is a small running stitch that goes through all three layers of the quilt. Take two, three, or even four stitches at a time if you can keep them even. When crossing seams, you might find it necessary to "hunt and peck" one stitch at a time.

To begin, insert the needle in the top layer about ¾" from the point where you want to start stitching. Pull the needle out at the starting point and gently tug at the knot until it pops through the fabric and is buried in the batting. Make a backstitch and begin quilting. Stitches should be tiny (8–10 per inch is good), even, and straight. At first, concentrate on even and straight; tiny will come with practice.

When you come almost to the end of the thread, make a single knot fairly close to the fabric. Make a backstitch to bury the knot in the batting. Run the thread off through the batting and out the quilt top. Snip it off. The first and last stitches look different from the running stitches between. To make them less noticeable, start and stop where quilting lines cross each other or at seam joints.

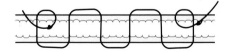

BINDING

MAKING BIAS STRIPS

Using a rotary cutter and mat, cut 2¼"-wide strips along the bias.

Seam ends together to make a continuous long strip. Fold fabric in half lengthwise, wrong sides together, and press. This will give you a double layer of bias binding. After sewing, both seam allowances will be on the front of the quilt, and the fold with no seam allowance will be on the back.

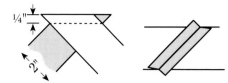

BINDING THE EDGES

After quilting, trim excess batting and backing even with the edge of the quilt top. A rotary cutter and long ruler will ensure accurate, straight edges. Baste all three layers together if basting from hand quilting is no longer in place.

1. Using a ¼"-wide seam allowance and beginning in the center of one side, sew the binding strip to the right side of the quilt, sewing through all layers. Be careful not to stretch the bias or the quilt edge as you sew. Stitch until you reach the seam-line intersection at the corner. Backstitch; cut threads.

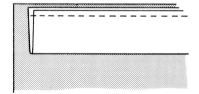

2. Turn quilt to prepare for sewing along the next edge. Fold the binding away from the quilt as shown, then fold again to place binding along edge of quilt. (This creates a right-angle fold at the corner.)

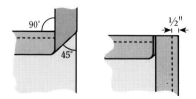

3. Stitch from fold of binding to seam line of adjacent edge. Backstitch; cut threads. Fold binding as in step 2 and continue around edge.

4. Join the beginning and ending of the binding strip, or plan to hand sew one end to overlap the other.

5. Turn binding to the back side and blindstitch in place. At each corner, fold binding in the sequence shown to form a miter on the back of the quilt.

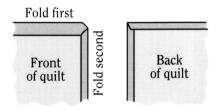

Cream-Cheese Foldovers

2 cups sifted all-purpose flour
¼ teaspoon salt
1 cup butter or margarine, softened
8 oz. cream cheese, softened
Confectioners' sugar
2 cups red jelly or jam

1. Preheat oven to 375° F.
2. Sift flour and salt together into bowl and set aside.
3. In large bowl of electric mixer, cream together softened butter and cream cheese until light and fluffy.
4. Blend in flour mixture.
5. Chill for several hours, or until firm enough to roll. Roll to ⅛" thickness on

Lemon Honey

1 cup sugar
¼ cup butter, chopped
Grated peel of 2 lemons
Juice of 3 lemons
3 eggs, beaten

1. In a heatproof bowl or top of double boiler, combine sugar, butter, lemon peel, and lemon juice.
2. Cook over low heat until butter melts, stirring occasionally.
3. Stir in eggs. Do not let mixture boil, or it will curdle. Continue stirring over low heat until mixture thickens.
4. Pour into sterilized jars, seal with a sterilized lid, and cool. Store in the refrigerator. It keeps up to 2 weeks. Use as a filling for flans or spread on bread and scones. Makes 2 cups.

Peach Clafouti

3 cups fresh peaches
1 tablespoon unsalted butter
½ cup sugar (or sugar substitute)
¾ cup evaporated skim milk
¼ cup nonfat milk
3 eggs
1 teaspoon vanilla extract
Pinch of salt
⅔ cup all-purpose flour

1. Preheat oven to 350° F.
2. Butter a 9"-diameter glass pie plate or a fluted porcelain tart dish. Dust the bottom with 1 teaspoon sugar.

Sour Cream Coffee Cake

1 cup (2 sticks) margarine
1¼ cups sugar
2 eggs
2 cups flour
1 tablespoon baking powder
½ teaspoon baking soda
1 cup sour cream
Filling (recipe follows)

1. Preheat oven to 350° F.
2. In large bowl of electric mixer, beat margarine and sugar together until creamy. Beat in eggs, one at a time; blend well.
3. Sift flour, baking powder, and soda together and add alternately with sour Cream

Cream Cheese Foldovers (cont.)

board sprinkled with confectioners' sugar. Cut in trapezoid shapes with knife, making shapes about 2" across widest side.

6. Spread with red jelly or jam. Fold over once so that sides meet. Place on greased cookie sheets.

7. Bake for about 15 minutes. (Do not allow to brown.) If desired, sprinkle with confectioners' sugar. Makes about 4 dozen.

Peach Clafouti (cont.)

3. In a blender, combine the evaporated skim milk, nonfat milk, eggs, remaining sugar, vanilla, salt, and flour. Blend at high speed for 1 minute, scraping the sides of the blender jar once.

4. Pour ½ cup of the batter into the dish. Arrange the peaches on top in an even layer. Pour remaining batter over the peaches.

5. Bake for 45 to 60 minutes, or until the top is puffed and golden brown and the batter is set. Serve warm. Serves 6.

Note: You may substitute other fresh fruits or berries for the peaches. Try apples, pears, sour cherries, blueberries, plums, nectarines, apricots, or cranberries.

Sour Cream Coffee Cake (cont.)

cream to creamed mixture, blending well after each addition.

4. Grease and flour a Bundt pan. Pour in ⅓ of the batter and add ½ the filling, more batter, remaining filling, and rest of batter.

5. Bake for 1 hour. Cool slightly before removing cake from pan.

Filling: Combine 5 tablespoons sugar, 2 teaspoons cinnamon, and ½ cup chopped nuts in a small bowl.

Strawberry Delight Cake

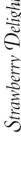

2½ cups sifted cake flour
1½ cups sugar
4 teaspoons double-acting baking powder
1 teaspoon salt
½ cup shortening
1 cup milk, divided
1 teaspoon vanilla
2 eggs
Strawberry Filling (recipe follows)
Snowy Cream Frosting (recipe follows)
Whole, fresh strawberries (optional)

1. Have ingredients at room temperature. Preheat oven to 375° F.
2. Line bottom of 2 jelly roll pans or cookie sheets with 2 layers of waxed paper.
3. Sift together flour, sugar, baking powder, and salt.
4. Add the shortening, ⅔ cup of the milk, and vanilla to dry ingredients in mixing bowl. Beat 2 minutes with mixer (or by hand using 150 strokes a minute). Scrape sides of bowl during mixing.
5. Add eggs and the remaining milk and beat 2 more minutes. Divide batter and spread evenly in the 2 pans. Bake about 15 minutes. Remove from oven. Cool slightly on racks, then invert on serving plate, remove cakes, and peel off paper.
6. Spread Strawberry Filling between cake layers and frost the top layer with Snowy Cream Frosting.
7. Decorate top with whole, fresh berries, if desired.

Buche de Noel (Yule Log)

Buche de Noel is made like a jelly roll, filled with a creamy filling, and decorated to resemble the bark of a tree.

5 eggs, separated
¼ teaspoon cream of tartar
1 cup granulated sugar
1 tablespoon grated orange rind
Coffee Cream Filling (recipe follows)
Chocolate Frosting (recipe follows)
2 tablespoons sherry
1 cup sifted cake flour
¼ teaspoon salt
Confectioners' sugar
Grated pistachio nuts
Marzipan (optional)

1. Preheat oven to 375° F.
2. Beat egg whites until foamy. Add cream of tartar and beat until stiff. Gradually beat in ½ cup of the granulated sugar, 1 tablespoon at a time.
3. Beat egg yolks until thick and lemon colored.
4. Beat remaining ½ cup granulated sugar, orange rind, and sherry into the egg yolks. Fold egg-yolk mixture into egg whites.
5. Sift flour with salt; fold gradually into egg mixture.
6. Pour into foil-lined jelly-roll pan (1" x 15" x 10"). Bake for about 20 minutes. Let cool in pan for 10 minutes.
7. Turn out on a towel sprinkled with confectioners' sugar. Carefully remove foil from cake.
8. From the shorter end, roll up cake in the towel and allow to stand until cold.
9. Unroll carefully and spread with Coffee Cream Filling.
10. Reroll and spread the entire roll with Chocolate Frosting. Run fork tines along the length of the cake to resemble bark.
11. Sprinkle grated pistachio nuts along the "bark" of the cake and trim with marzipan leaves, if desired. Serves 8–10.

Strawberry Delight Cake (cont.)

Strawberry Filling

Combine two 10-ounce packages of frozen strawberries, thawed (or 2 quarts fresh), ¼ cup cornstarch (more for fresh berries), ¼ teaspoon salt, ½ cup sugar, ¼ cup water, and 1 tablespoon butter in medium saucepan. Cook and stir over low heat until mixture is clear and thick. Cool.

Snowy Cream Frosting

Cream ½–⅓ cup butter. Add 2–2½ cups sifted confectioners' sugar, 4 tablespoons milk or cream, and 1 teaspoon vanilla. Cream together and beat until smooth and creamy, adding confectioners' sugar as needed for spreading consistency.

Buche de Noel (cont.)

Coffee Cream Filling

Combine 2 cups heavy cream with ¼ cup confectioners' sugar and 1 tablespoon instant coffee powder and chill for 2 or more hours. Whip until thick enough to spread.

Chocolate Frosting

Melt 3 ounces (3 squares) unsweetened chocolate and 3 tablespoons butter or margarine. Mix 4 cups confectioners' sugar, ⅛ teaspoon salt, 7 tablespoons milk, and 1 teaspoon vanilla. Add chocolate mixture and blend well. Let stand, stirring occasionally, until of spreading consistency.

Chocolate-Covered Strawberries

36 large, fresh strawberries
1 cup semi-sweet chocolate chips
2 teaspoons vegetable oil

1. Wash strawberries; gently pat dry.
2. Line a tray with waxed paper.
3. In small saucepan over low heat, melt chocolate chips and vegetable oil, stirring occasionally until smooth. Remove from heat. Set saucepan in pan of hot water to maintain dipping consistency.
4. Dip strawberries into chocolate mixture until the lower ⅔ of each strawberry is coated. Allow excess chocolate to drip off; place strawberries, stem side down, on paper-lined tray.
5. Refrigerate until serving time. Makes 36.

Sour Cream Dip for Strawberries

1 cup sour cream
2 tablespoons sugar (or sugar substitute)

1. Combine sour cream and sugar. Chill.
2. Serve with fresh strawberries or other fruit.

Teacup Petits Fours

1 package white cake mix with pudding included
¼ cup vegetable oil
3 egg whites
3 cups confectioners' sugar
3 tablespoons light corn syrup
2 tablespoons margarine or butter, melted
½ teaspoon vanilla extract
¼ teaspoon almond extract
Frosting, tinted pink and blue
Decorating bag and tips

1. Preheat oven to 350° F. Grease and flour 1" x 10" x 15" baking pan.
2. In large bowl, combine cake mix, 1¼ cups water, vegetable oil, and egg whites.

Langue de Chat (Cat's Tongue) Cookies

¼ cup butter
¼ cup sifted sugar
2 eggs
1 teaspoon vanilla
½ cup sifted all-purpose flour

Note: These require special ladyfinger-shaped pans.
1. Preheat oven to 350° F. Grease molds.
2. Cream butter and sifted sugar.
3. Beat in eggs and vanilla.
4. Fold in flour.
5. Bake 15 minutes. Serve with chocolate icing for dipping. Makes 2 dozen.

Teacup Petits Fours (cont.)

Mix at low speed until moistened, then beat 2 minutes at high speed.

3. Pour batter into prepared baking pan. Bake for 20–30 minutes, or until toothpick inserted in center comes out clean; cool.

4. To avoid cake crumbs, freeze cake 1 hour before cutting. Cut into pieces, using teacup template on page 16. (Trace template and cut from heavy paper or light-weight cardboard.) Place pattern on cake and cut around it with a sharp knife.

5. In small bowl, combine confectioners' sugar, ¼ cup water, corn syrup, marga-rine, and extracts at low speed until sugar is moistened. Beat at high speed until smooth. If necessary, add 2–3 teaspoons water until icing is desired consistency. Spoon icing evenly over top and sides of cake cutouts. (Icing that drips off can be reused.)

6. Using tinted frosting, outline and decorate shapes to look like patterned china. Makes 20–24.